PERSONAL FINANCE FOR TEENS

THE INDEPENDENCE BLUEPRINT

MASTER INCOME, EXPENSES & SIDE HUSTLING,
LEARN TO SAVE, INVEST AND BUDGET TO BECOME
FINANCIALLY INDEPENDENT

J.L. DAVIS

CONTENTS

INTRODUCTION

We all have a friend who often worries about money, telling us their troubles while enjoying a $6 Starbucks coffee. Starbucks three times a week at $6 a pop—that's $936 per year! But have you ever considered that they, like many of us, might simply lack the right guidance on managing finances? Research shows that 74% of teens in the U.S. do not think they know enough about finances, and 32% of teens do not know the difference between a credit and debit card (Darko Jacimovic, 2022). I wrote this book for teens just like you, transforming the confusion around money into clear, fun, and empowering lessons.

Schools often neglect to teach teens the basics of handling money and finances, yet they are expected to have knowledge about taxes, investments, insurance, and compound interest when they graduate. In this book, we simplify complex financial concepts into understandable and actionable steps, empowering you to confidently manage and make the most of your finances. You will learn exactly how to transform that $936 you're saving from eliminating Starbucks three times a week to make a whopping $166,054 for your future! Get ready to turn those coffee chats into savvy financial discussions and master the art of making your money work for you!

This book is an easy-to-follow roadmap to financial independence. We will guide you through each step, ensuring you have the knowledge and tools to confidently navigate your financial journey. Here's what we have in store for you:

- **Unlock the Vault of Financial Wisdom**: Like a treasure map leading to hidden gold, this book will guide you through the labyrinth of financial literacy, help you avoid common pitfalls, and unlock the untapped potential of your finances.
- **Craft Your Financial Armor**: By mastering having a financial mindset, budgeting, and smart spending, you will learn the mental and tactical tools needed to navigate the battleground of modern economics—armor against a world of unpredictable challenges.
- **Turn Pennies into Power**: We will introduce you to the alchemy of investing and compound interest. You will discover how to transform your modest savings into burgeoning portfolios, crafting the recipe that turns pocket change into financial freedom.
- **Navigate the Mirage**: This book will navigate the mirage of a world dazzling with consumer temptations, enabling you to recognize fleeting illusions and genuine needs to walk through the fires of consumerism without getting burned.
- **Become Financially Resilient**: From side hustles to emergency funds, the book teaches how to bend but not break under financial pressure. It's not just about earning

or saving; it's about learning to weather storms with finesse.

- **Give Back**: In the last lap of the financial marathon, we will show you how you can give back to humanity while you are building your financial empire.

Imagine that after reading this book, you start to implement the steps we suggest. You create a realistic budget and start to save for the things that are important to you. You begin to side hustle and take on a part-time job, and by the time you finish high school, you don't need to take out student loans to pay for your college education. While you are studying, you continue with the financial habits you have learned from reading this book, and soon after you start your first job, you are able to start living an abundant life. You can soon afford to buy the car and home of your dreams, and if you choose, a family can follow. You will be able to live a life filled with the things you dream about now.

For many people, these dreams will stay just that—dreams. But you will start to take control of your financial destiny today. You are the exception to the rule, and we will guide you step-by-step.

PILLAR 1

MINDSET MASTERY

The most important investment you can make is in yourself.

— WARREN BUFFET

1

BILLIONAIRE BRAINWAVES: SHAPING YOUR FINANCIAL DESTINY

Imagine being an alchemist, the cool kind from old tales, mixing science and philosophy to turn regular metals into precious gold. Now, think of this chapter as your lab, where we will transform how you think about money, unlocking its amazing potential. It is like mixing different ingredients to brew an elixir for success. We will blend ideas like the "fixed vs. growth" mindset and "scarcity vs. abundance" views to cook up a powerful recipe for financial success.

Understanding and adopting these principles at a young age is not just a smart move; it can change your financial destiny. In this chapter, we will go beyond just managing money. We will look at how developing the right mindset and gaining important insights can set you up for a lifetime of financial independence. So, let's set out on the exciting process of transforming your goals into gold!

Unlocking the Secret Chamber: Why Mindset Matters

Before we start our discussion on a healthy money mindset, let me tell you about Linda and how she beat the odds on her journey to financial independence. Her secret was that her mindset was right.

Linda grew up in a normal neighborhood in a normal suburb, where dreams seemed unimportant against her daily struggles. While her family did not have a lot of money, they were rich in love and determination, two skills that Linda found very valuable throughout her life. As a young girl, Linda realized that she would have to do things differently if she wanted her financial circumstances to change. She knew that financial independence was her ticket to making a difference in her family's life and her community. With grit and determination, Linda decided to learn as much as she could about what she needed to do to make her dreams come true. So, Linda read all the financial articles and books she could get her hands on. Although she often encountered unfamiliar terms and strange financial jargon, Linda remained determined to learn and could frequently be seen conducting research on her tablet to better understand the challenging topics.

Early in high school, Linda started her first side hustle, walking dogs, and she found a part-time waiter job at a coffee shop. She saved diligently for her college education as she realized she would need to take out expensive student loans to make this happen. During the time that Linda was working and saving, she often had to face criticism from her friends, who could not understand why Linda would not spend her hard-earned money on cool gadgets or use some of it to join them when they went out over weekends. But she persevered with the determination she had been taught, maintaining her unwavering focus and resilient mindset. She kept learning about finances and investments and believed that this one day would change her life.

And she was right! Linda's hard work at school earned her a full scholarship to a prestigious college. She used some of the money she saved over the years to buy all the little things her scholarship did not pay for, the bulk of which she invested with the help of a financial advisor who also became her financial mentor. After college, Linda pursued her dream of becoming an entrepreneur, and all the financial knowledge she learned over the years came in handy to start her own business. With hard work and determination, Linda was able to build her business into a flourishing company, and soon, she was employing other people to work for her.

Today, Linda is a well-respected businesswoman. She owns her own home and drives a nifty sports coupe. She is still practicing healthy money habits and has enough money saved and invested that she does not need to worry about retirement. But Linda has not forgotten where she started; she has set up a financial aid plan for children in her area who do not have the money to pay for college, and she is a regular volunteer at her old high school to teach kids about financial literacy.

Now, it is your turn to discover the alchemy of financial independence, just as Linda did. In this chapter, we will explore the mindset and strategies that can turn your dreams into reality too, no matter where you start.

FIXED VS. GROWTH MINDSET

The way you think about money, your "money mindset," is a powerful tool that can either help you become successful or keep you stuck where you are forever. Let's look at some characteristics of each mindset and find out how you can change yours.

Fixed Mindset

With a fixed mindset, you are trapped inside a box, believing that your abilities, talents, and intelligence are unchangeable and that whatever you do, "it is what it is." You might think, "I am either good at something or I am not." Challenges can feel overwhelming, and you might avoid them because you are afraid of failing. People with this mindset may also believe that they know everything there is to know about a subject and don't need to learn anymore. They are often envious and feel threatened by the success of others, and they think of excuses for why they are not successful or downplay the other person's success.

Meet Phil, a high school student who has always believed that one's home circumstances determine financial success. His family has suffered financially for as long as he can remember, and he grew up hearing comments like "We are not the kind of people who can afford that" or "Money is just not on our side." As a result, Phil has developed a fixed-money mindset. He is convinced that no matter how hard he works or how hard he tries, he will never be financially secure. When he sees friends who appear to effortlessly afford the latest technology or go on expensive vacations, he simply thinks to himself, "That is just not in the cards for someone like me." This mindset keeps Phil from finding opportunities, taking smart financial risks, or simply believing in his ability to better his financial situation. He is trapped in a cycle of limiting beliefs that stifle his financial growth because he believes that his background determines his financial future. Luckily, Phil and everyone else with a fixed mindset can break free from these negative beliefs and learn how to develop a growth mindset that allows them to take charge of their own financial futures, no matter their starting point.

Growth Mindset

With a growth mindset, you believe that hard work, continuous learning, and determination can develop your abilities, talents, and intelligence. You see challenges as learning opportunities and setbacks as lessons, and you keep going, no matter what. It is like saying, "I can't do it...yet." A growth mindset also makes you more accepting of valid criticism; you are willing to do some introspection and make the necessary changes. People with this mindset are not envious of those who are more successful but want to learn from them.

A growth mindset is the key that unlocks your potential and propels you forward on the path of financial freedom. It is all about seeing challenges as stepping stones, being willing to learn, and having the resilience to overcome financial obstacles.

According to a recent article, more than three out of four Americans, or 77%, feel anxious about money, finances, and the future, and 58% feel that finances control their lives (White, 2020). These are huge numbers. Consider this: Finances stress three out of four people. The good news is that you don't need to be one of them; if you learn to have a growth mindset and practice the strategies we will share with you in this book, you will be well on your way to success. And you are never too young to start. Remember Linda from the story above? By starting early, she was able to make smart choices from the start and avoid big and costly mistakes.

But let's be honest: You are going to face some financial challenges in your life, and you will need to choose to see every challenge as an opportunity to learn and grow. If you want to buy a new gadget but don't have the funds, you can either say, "I was just not meant to have it," or you can start making a plan by looking for part-time job opportunities or finding out how you can adjust your budget to save more. Once you take charge of your finances, endless possibilities await!

Tips to Change From a Fixed to a Growth Mindset

- **Believe in the power of "yet"**: Replace thoughts like "I can't do this" with "I can't do this *yet*." The word "yet" tells you that with effort, you can grow and improve over time.
- **Embrace challenges**: Don't be scared of challenges, but rather think of them as opportunities to flex your financial muscles.
- **Learn from mistakes**: Instead of seeing mistakes as failures, see them as lessons well learned, move on, and don't repeat the same mistake twice.
- **Celebrate effort**: Reward yourself for hard work, dedication, and perseverance, not just for results. Your effort is an important part of the journey.
- **Be kind to yourself**: It is okay not to know everything. Everyone has to start somewhere, and moving forward with a willingness to learn is way more important than perfection.
- **Visualize your success**: Imagine yourself achieving your financial goals and living your dream life. Make this as real as you can—think of the color of the car you want to buy, or imagine the sand between your toes if a vacation is one of your goals. This will keep you motivated!

Changing your mindset will not happen overnight; you will need to keep working on it, but the reward is a brighter financial future!

SCARCITY VS. ABUNDANCE MINDSET

Apart from growth and fixed mindsets, we also need to look at scarcity and abundance mindsets. These two mindsets are two different ways to look at the same reality and, more specifically, finance, and they can greatly impact your financial journey.

Scarcity Mindset

This mindset is all about the fear that there are not enough resources (like money) to go around for everyone. When you have this mindset, you tend to focus on what you lack. You might worry about running out of money, missing out on opportunities, or not being able to afford the things you want. This can lead people to feel trapped, like they are on a sinking ship with limited resources. And of course, this can easily lead to feeling stressed and making decisions based on fear. And what little they have, they hoard. These people are not likely to share the little they believe they have with anyone else.

Abundance Mindset

On the other hand, an abundance mindset is all about believing that there is more than enough to go around. People with an abundance mindset see opportunities everywhere, and they believe in their ability to create wealth and abundance in their lives. They focus on possibilities and believe that there are plenty of opportunities to seize them. And, of course, if you believe there is enough for everyone, you don't mind sharing what you have.

What do these mindsets mean for your financial journey?

If you think about your finances with a scarcity mindset, you might constantly worry about not having enough money. This can lead to feelings of anxiety, which may cause you to be afraid to take even smart or calculated risks, which in turn may mean missed opportunities. For example, you may be too scared to invest your money in stocks but prefer to keep it in a savings account where it is safe but earns very little interest. Having an abundance mindset, on the other hand, can empower you to look for opportunities, take smart financial risks, and make investments that lead to financial success. It helps you see potential where others might only see problems.

Tips to Change From a Scarcity to an Abundance Mindset

Once you understand the different mindsets, we can start our exciting adventure to make sure you have an abundance mindset. It is like trading an old map for a new, exciting one filled with possibilities. To make these changes, follow these steps:

- **Set clear financial goals**: Imagine your goals as the treasure you are seeking on this new map. Set precise goals, like saving for a dream vacation, buying a new piece of technology, or even setting up a business. These goals will motivate you to keep at them, even when things are tough.
- **Embrace a learning adventure**: Think of financial education as your compass on the road to financial success. Learn about budgeting, saving, investing, and the power of compound interest. The more you understand money, the more control and confidence you will have.
- **Celebrate every step**: Treat each achievement as an important destination on your map. When you make progress, celebrate it! It could be as simple as a takeaway coffee; this positivity motivates you on your journey and builds momentum.
- **Practice gratitude**: Gratitude is like the wind filling your sails. Take a moment each day to appreciate what you have,

no matter how small it seems. This positivity attracts more abundance into your life.

- **Visualize success**: Imagine your success as a vivid destination on your map. Picture yourself achieving your goals. These visions of your future can motivate you and make your dreams feel more real.
- **Stay open to new opportunities**: Keep your eyes open for hidden treasures along the way. Be open to new things! It may be a new way of earning money, making smart investments, or finding new solutions to financial challenges.
- **Share your journey**: Just as it is better to travel with companions, share your financial goals with someone you trust. They can encourage and advise you and even join you on your adventure.
- **Learn from setbacks**: Think of setbacks as temporary detours. Financial challenges are opportunities to learn and grow. These challenging moments are important parts of your journey, as they teach you skills like thinking creatively and how to persevere.
- **Be patient and persistent**: This journey may have twists and turns. It is not about speed but all about determination. Keep moving forward, even when obstacles arise. Persistence pays off in the end.
- **Believe in your abilities**: Ultimately, it is your belief in abundance that will make the most important difference. Know that you have the power to create the life you want and that financial success is not only possible but just around the corner.
- **Celebrate the successes of others**: An abundance mindset means that you believe there is enough for everyone. Someone else being successful does not take away from your own success! By supporting, encouraging, and

celebrating each other's successes, our journey becomes more meaningful for everyone.

With clear goals, an open mindset, and the determination to learn and grow, you are well on your way to achieving financial abundance and realizing your dreams. Keep following your new map; the treasure of abundance is yours to discover!

Sculpting Your Financial Identity: Action Steps for Mindset Mastery

Here are some exercises that can help you grow a positive money mindset:

Gratitude Journaling

Start a gratitude journal where you write down things you are thankful for every day, including things about your finances. This practice can shift your focus from scarcity to abundance. You can write things like, "I am grateful for my allowance" or "I am thankful for the opportunity to save for my dream." When you start to focus on the positive things about your financial situation, your mindset will become more positive too.

Visualization and Goal Setting

Take time to paint a picture in your mind of your financial goals. Then imagine what it would feel like when you achieved them. If you are saving for a dream island holiday, imagine you can smell the suntan lotion and feel the sand between your toes. When you do this, it helps to make your financial dreams more real and exciting, which makes them easier to achieve. So take the time to visualize your dreams!

Money Saving Challenges

Challenge yourself and play this money-saving real-life game. Decide on something you really want but need to save for. Then, decide on a percentage of your income that you are going to save towards this goal. For example, you can challenge yourself to save 20% of your allowance each month. These challenges teach discipline, delayed gratification, and the satisfaction of achieving your financial goals through regular saving. Every time you are successful, it is like completing a challenge in a video game, and this will help your confidence and positive mindset grow.

But you have to remember that creating a better money mindset takes time and practice. Just like a sculptor carefully shapes a masterpiece from a block of marble, if you consistently practice these steps, you can chisel away at an unhelpful mindset and set yourself on a path to financial success.

Now that you understand how mastering your mindset is the first step in your journey to financial success, we can explore the next step. In the next chapter, we will discover a different kind of magic thinking: that of becoming mindful and developing your emotional intelligence.

2

MINDFULNESS AND MONEY—THE HEARTBEAT OF EMOTIONAL INTELLIGENCE

Have you ever wondered if being in control of your emotions could be the secret to financial success? It seems that your heart and wallet are more closely connected than you might think. In this chapter, we will delve into the important and often overlooked relationship between your emotions and your finances. We will see how your thoughts, feelings, and actions can either propel you toward financial success or hold you back in a cycle of stress and anxiety.

HOW EMOTIONAL INTELLIGENCE CONTROLS MONEY MANAGEMENT

Picture this: It is a bright, sunny day, and Maddy, a high school senior with big dreams, is on the verge of making her first big financial decision—buying her first car. She has been saving diligently from her part-time job for months, and she can feel the open road calling. As she walks into the sleek, modern showroom, her heart racing, and her palms sweaty, she is bouncing with excitement. The shiny, but expensive, sports car in front of her immediately catches her eye, and the salesperson's promises of speed and style are music in her ears. Maddy imagines herself behind the wheel, turning heads and living life in the fast lane. But here is the catch: this dream car comes at a cost that pushes the limits of her budget. Maddy's friends have cars; her social media is filled with pictures of friends and their rides; and she is afraid of missing out. As the salesperson sweetens the deal with financing options, Maddy's emotions begin to cloud her judgment. She starts to think, "Why not go for it? I worked hard, and I deserve it." And right there, Maddy made a financial decision that will haunt her for many years to come. By committing to more than she could afford, she started a downward spiral where she was struggling to keep up with the car payments for a long time. It took many years for Maddy to get out of debt, and once she did, she promised herself never to make a big financial decision again based on emotions but rather on logic.

EMOTIONAL INTELLIGENCE EXPLAINED

Emotional intelligence has five pillars, and each of these pillars can affect the way you manage your financial decisions (Cherry, 2023). Let's break down the key components of EQ and see how they can impact your wallet.

Self-Awareness

This is all about understanding your own emotions and realizing how they can affect your money choices. For instance, being aware of your tendency to overspend when stressed or sad allows you to prevent unnecessary splurges.

Self-Regulation

This is the ability to manage your emotions and not let them control your financial decisions. Self-regulation means not buying that gadget just because you are feeling down; it will not make you feel better. It is realizing that you are not in a good space and finding healthy ways (like talking to someone or going for a walk) to actually make you feel better.

Social Awareness

EQ also includes understanding others' emotions. This can be crucial when, for instance, you are negotiating a raise or a business deal. It also means understanding peer pressure and having the self-control not to give in to it. Just because all your friends have the newest iPhone doesn't mean you need one too!

Motivation

When you have strong financial motivation, you are more likely to save, invest, and make smart money decisions. It is the part that keeps you going, even when the road to financial independence gets tough. If you are motivated to save for a certain item, you will be less likely to give in to impulse spending and use your savings for something else.

Empathy

Empathy is all about understanding and connecting with other people's feelings. For example, imagine you and your friend are planning a trip together. You know your friend is on a tight budget, but you want to stay in a fancy hotel. By putting yourself in your friend's shoes and understanding their financial situation, you choose a more budget-friendly hotel, which means both of you can enjoy the holiday without stressing about money. This decision shows empathy by considering your friend's feelings, which will strengthen your friendship and make the trip more enjoyable for both of you.

The Link Between EQ and Financial Success

In the business world, emotional intelligence (EQ) is very important. According to a recent study, EQ skills are responsible for 85% of financial success (Miller, 2018). People with high EQ tend to make rational and less emotional financial decisions. They can assess risks and rewards more effectively, which can lead to better investment choices and financial planning.

Another interesting study links how much people earn to their EQ. The study looked at 42,000 people from all industries, at all levels, and in every region of the world. Some shocking results came out of the study. The results showed that 90% of top workers are emotionally intelligent and that these people also make $29,000 more a year on average than people who are less emotionally intelligent. The study also showed that there is such a strong link between EQ and salary that each EQ point boosts your early salary by $1,300 per year (Islam, 2021).

To put it simply, EQ can help you make smart financial choices, stay on track with your money, and build important financial relationships. It is not just about numbers; it is also about how EQ can help you get around the complicated world of money. It is like having a superpower that helps you read maps that other people find challenging.

THE CURRENCY OF SELF-CONTROL: HOW EMOTIONAL RESTRAINT EQUALS FINANCIAL GAIN

Self-control is like the vigilant guardian at the gateway of your financial kingdom. Making sure that your hard-earned treasures remain safe from the reckless raids of emotional whims. It prevents you from succumbing to the temptation of purchasing something solely because others are spending money on it.

Riders, Elephants, and Your Money

In the book *Switch,* they use a brilliant analogy that imagines that within each of us, there are two characters: a "rider" and an "elephant." The rider represents the logical, analytical self—the one that plans, thinks ahead, and makes rational decisions. It knows that saving money for future goals, like a car or college, is essential. The elephant, on the other hand, symbolizes your emotional, impulsive self. The elephant acts on immediate desires and emotions. It might see something exciting or enticing (like a peanut advertisement on Instagram) and want it right now (Heath Brothers, 2013). Typically, what the elephant wants, it gets.

The key point here is that even if the rider knows that certain decisions are bad for your long-term financial goals, the elephant's desires can often be too strong to resist. It is the emotional side that wants us to make impulsive purchases or spurges. The challenge is to learn how to control your "elephant," or emotional self. By understanding this internal struggle, you can develop strategies and techniques to help the rider guide the elephant in the right direction, ensuring that your financial decisions fit with your long-term goals. It is about finding a balance between logic and emotion to make sound financial choices.

The Trap We Face

Companies invest billions of dollars in social media advertising, and their goal is to convince you that you need their products or services. They are experts at understanding human behavior and psychology, and they use this knowledge to break down your self-control bit by bit. This can make it challenging to resist their enticing offers and advertisements. But if you know about the trap, you don't need to step into it! You have the power to stay in control. Once you can see through the illusion and see the tactics for what they are, you can be mindful of your own impulses. Understanding that these ads tap into your emotions and desires allows you to make conscious choices about your spending.

The Holiday Savings Dilemma

Emily had been saving for a dream holiday for years. One day, she saw the most amazing photographs of an island holiday that was just outside of her budget. It would have meant making debt to afford it, and Emily decided to sleep on it before making a decision. In the bright sunlight, the holiday pictures did not look so tempting, especially once she realized how long she would be paying off the debt she would have to make. So Emily exercised self-control and continued saving, and eventually, she found a better deal on an even better holiday that fit her budget without putting strain on her finances—she even had enough money to buy gifts for everyone at home!

The Online Shopping Temptation

Jake received his first paycheck, and after seeing an advertisement for a new gaming console, he was very tempted to splurge. But in the car on his way back home, Jake talked about it with his older brother, who explained that he would be using all of his savings. His brother advised him to wait a week before spending such a large amount. Jake took his brother's advice and exercised self-control by waiting and doing some more research. During that time, he reconsidered and decided to prioritize saving for college.

The Sneaker Savings Lesson

Taylor had a passion for collecting sneakers. One day, she stumbled upon a limited edition pair that was selling at a hefty price. Instead of making an impulsive purchase, she exercised self-control and did her research. She discovered that the same pair was available for a more reasonable price from a different source, making her thankful for not buying on impulse.

Digital Temptation: Navigating the FOMO Trap on Social Media

Imagine you are scrolling through your Instagram feed, and your friends are all posting pictures of their latest gadgets, trendy clothes, and amazing vacations. You see them having the time of their lives, and the fear of missing out begins to creep in. Your favorite clothing brand is having a limited-time sale, and the influencer you follow is promoting a new must-have accessory. Everyone is buying things and living their best lives, and you don't want to be left out.

Instagram and other social media apps capture your attention and keep you scrolling. They spend billions of dollars to create a world where everything seems perfect, and everyone appears to be living their dream life. This curated version of reality can make it difficult to keep your self-control by making you want things you didn't even know you wanted. These apps can be a vortex of temptation, continually bombarding you with advertisements, deals, and influencers promoting products. FOMO is a powerful emotional force that can lead to impulse purchases. By understanding that the images you see on social media are often not a true reflection of real life, you can practice self-control and resist the urge to make impulsive purchases.

Practicing Exercises for Self-Control

Imagine yourself as the captain of a ship sailing through choppy waters. Let's look at a few tools to help you navigate your financial ship successfully.

The Pause Button Technique

When you feel the urge to make an impulse purchase, stop and take a deep breath. Imagine hitting the pause button in your mind. Then, ask yourself a few questions: Do I really need this item? Can I afford it without going into debt or sacrificing my savings goals? Will it still make me happy in a few months, or is it just something I want for now?

Then, wait for a day or two before making the purchase. During this time, you may decide that this is not the best option for you, or you may feel convinced that it is something you need.

The Mindful Spending Journal

Think of your financial journey as a map and this exercise as a compass.

Here is how it works:

- Get a small notebook or use a note-taking app on your phone.
- Every time you buy something, write down what you bought, why you bought it, and how it made you feel.
- At the end of each week, look at the things you bought. Can you see any patterns? Are there emotional triggers that make you spend money?

- Use this journal to help you make smarter spending choices by understanding your spending habits better.

Mindful Apps for Financial Clarity

There are many budgeting apps that can help you navigate your financial ship; these include Mint, YNAB (You Need a Budget), or PocketGuard.

Connect your bank accounts and set financial goals within the app. These apps are like navigational instruments, showing you where your money is going and helping you stay on track.

LIVING CHRONICLES: TALES OF EMOTIONAL INTELLIGENCE IN ACTION

Elle Kaplan, CEO of LXION

Meet Elle Kaplan, the CEO of LXION Capital, who is a strong advocate for the power of emotional intelligence (EQ) in achieving financial success. She believes that EQ is a good predictor of future financial success, and she shares the following traits that successful individuals share (Kaplan, 2018).

- **Take control of your emotions: Warren Buffet** famously said, "If you can't control your emotions, you can't control your money" (Kaplan, 2018). One of the things that can sink your financial ship is emotional spending, and by being able to manage your emotions, you can avoid this trap. Buffet advises using the 10:10:10 method before spending money. Ask yourself, "How will this make me feel after 10 minutes, 10 months, and 10 years?"

- **Ask questions**: This tip refers to a growth mindset. **Steve Jobs** more than once referred to "curiosity" as one of the reasons for his success (Turak, 2011). Curiosity drives you to try new things, to learn, and to explore different ways of doing things. By being curious, you can spot opportunities and keep improving your skills.
- **Self-discipline**: Remember Jiminy Cricket in the Pinocchio story? You also have that little voice in your head telling you what to do or what to avoid. Remember, the decisions you make today will have an impact on your financial future.
- **Practice empathy**: According to **Oprah Winfrey**, empathy improves your chances of being successful (Harvard Business School, 2020). No one is an island; we all need a support system (and to offer our support) to be successful.
- **Ask for help**: Don't be scared to ask for help from people who are already successful. Starbucks founder **Howard Schultz**'s advice is to surround yourself with people who are smarter than you and then learn from them (Long, 2014).

Emotional Intelligence in Banking

Did you know that banks are getting smarter about emotions too? Yep, they are not just about numbers and dollars anymore. Now, they are adding emotional intelligence to their banking experiences. Banks are starting to understand that money is about dreams, goals, and feelings tied to it, and they now try to incorporate these into their banking experiences.

By intuitively knowing what their customers struggle with, they are able to give them the answers they need even before they ask them. To do this, they need to understand their customers' needs, dreams, and financial goals. They collect a bunch of data about your spending habits, your account history, and more. They are then able to use this data to offer you personalized services. For example, if you have been saving up for a trip to Disneyland, they might suggest a special savings account just for that. These personalized features are designed to enhance your banking experience.

Financial Leaders on EQ

Let's look at the big bosses in the financial world—the successful ones who really get how people feel and act. They shared some of their secrets in a recent article (Bushee, 2022).

- **They understand themselves**: These leaders are super aware of their own emotions and actions.
- **They lead with empathy**: Because they know themselves so well, they can lead others with finesse. It is like they have a magical power to guide and inspire their teams.
- **They create awesome teams**: These leaders are like super team-builders. They bring people together and make everyone feel positive and motivated.

These leaders have discovered that EI is a superpower; it helps their business grow, keeps their employees happy, attracts more customers, and makes sure everyone sticks around for the long haul. They are financial superheroes!

EQ Creates Successful CEOs

Let's have a look at how some very successful CEOs use EQ to become even more successful:

- **Elon Musk** understands that actions speak louder than words. According to a recent article, he offered to work alongside factory workers to really understand their challenges (Mejia, 2017).
- PepsiCo's CEO, **Indra Nooyi**, believes in saying "thank you" and is known for her handwritten thank-you notes to employees. By acknowledging and valuing them as individuals, she has been able to bond with her team in a personal way; she believes this has played a huge part in her success (David Rubenstein Show, 2016).
- **Jack Welch**, former chairman and CEO of General Motors, believes in having a growth mindset for success. He recalls making a mistake as a young staff member and how this forced him to take responsibility for his actions, but it was also an opportunity to find innovative solutions —a skill that propelled him to success.

Growing your EQ is not like a one-time video game you beat and move on; it is more like an ongoing adventure, kind of like your favorite Netflix series. In this journey, you will face many challenges; there may be moments when your emotions may get the best of you, and that is okay! These challenges can help you grow even faster. And there will be moments when you handle tough situations like a pro or when you connect with someone in a way that makes you both feel awesome. Therefore, embrace the challenges and savor the triumphs along the way, as they are integral to your journey of becoming the awesome person you are meant to be!

Now that you have learned to tune into your emotions, are you ready to unlock the bank vaults and explore some practical ways to master your finances?

PILLAR 2

THE FOUNDATIONS OF YOUR FINANCIAL FORTRESS

Do not save what is left after spending, but spend what is left after saving.

— WARREN BUFFET

3

THE BANK VAULT

Think of a bank as a tool, not just a vault. Today, we'll dissect the anatomy of various accounts and unearth how each can be a gear in your wealth-building machine.

Imagine stepping into a world where the essence of financial security and stability is palpable—welcome to the bank vault. This isn't just any ordinary space; it is a fortress, a sanctum of fiscal responsibility. These walls, gleaming under the soft fluorescent lights, are not just barriers; they are guardians of wealth, silently vowing to protect what lies within. As we discover more about this financial tool, it is time to embark on a journey through the various types of bank accounts.

Checking Accounts: The Daily Essentials

First, we have the checking account. This is the workhorse of the banking world, a staple in personal finance. Think of it as the everyday wallet of banking accounts. Checking accounts are designed for everyday transactions such as receiving your paycheck, paying bills, or withdrawing cash. A checking account is easy to access, straightforward, functional, and a basic account to have for most people. But they also have their limits. While they offer convenience, they don't grow your money. Checking accounts earn little to no interest, reminding us that they are not suitable for long-term investments.

Savings Accounts: The Quiet Growth Chambers

Next, let's talk about how savings accounts can help your money grow more quickly. These accounts offer a safe space for your money to grow, although at a slow pace. The interest rates here are higher than checking accounts, making them a good choice for short-term goals or emergency funds. Savings accounts come with their own set of rules and limitations; for example, there is a limit to how often you can withdraw from them without paying fees. This restriction, while sometimes inconvenient, serves a purpose: it keeps your money safely growing until you really need it.

Certificates of Deposit (CDs): The Timed Exhibits

Certificates of Deposit are like the beta versions of games; they are only available for a specific duration. When you open a CD, you agree to leave your money untouched for a fixed period, which could range from a few months to several years. In return, you are offered a higher interest rate compared to savings accounts. The catch with CDs is their inflexibility. Withdrawing money before the term ends can result in penalties, meaning you miss out on earning the full amount of interest. CDs are ideal for those who have a clear timeline for their financial goals and can afford to set aside money for a fixed period.

Money Market Accounts: The Versatile Displays

Finally, we come to money market accounts. These are versatile accounts that offer higher interest rates than CDs but with the added benefit of check-writing and debit card access, much like checking accounts. They strike a balance between earning potential and liquidity. However, money market accounts often require a higher minimum balance compared to other accounts, and the interest rates can fluctuate.

Each type of account serves a unique purpose in the grand scheme of financial literacy and stability. Your banking portfolio can benefit from a diverse collection of accounts, each playing its role in safeguarding and growing our financial resources. Remember, in the world of finance, knowledge is not just power—it is profit!

THE GRAND CEREMONY OF OPENING A BANK ACCOUNT

Embarking on the journey of opening a bank account is like participating in a grand financial ceremony, a rite of passage into the world of monetary wisdom and responsibility. For those under 18, this process requires a bit of teamwork, as you will need to open a "custodial account." This means that you will need to involve a parent or guardian. This partnership is not only a legal requirement, but it is also an opportunity for you to learn and grow under the guidance of someone more experienced in the world of finance.

Let's see what you need to open your first bank account.

Step 1: Gathering of Tools

The first step is to gather your personal identification documents. You will need your Social Security number, a photo ID (like a school ID or a passport), and maybe proof of address (like a utility bill or a bank statement).

Step 2: Choosing Your Financial Sanctuary

Next, you must choose the right financial institution—your bank or credit union. Research different banks and credit unions; focus on those that offer teen-friendly account options. Consider factors like minimum balance requirements, fees, interest rates, and accessibility. This step is about finding a financial sanctuary that resonates with your needs and values—a place where your money will be safe and can grow.

Step 3: Apply for Your Account

You can fill out the account application online or in person at a branch. During the account application process, you need to provide your personal information and decide on the type of account you want to open. A good starting point is a checking account and a savings account.

Step 4: Deposit Your First Funds

Now comes the moment when you make your first deposit into the account. This could be money from your savings, a gift from a family member, or your earnings from a part-time job. This act represents your commitment and the start of your journey toward building financial stability.

Step 5: Receiving the Tools of Access

Once your account is open, you will receive the tools of access—your debit card and online banking credentials. Your debit card and online banking access give you the power to manage your finances, track your spending, and grow your savings. Treat these tools with respect and mindfulness, for they are important for your financial autonomy.

Step 6: Your First Financial Transactions

When you engage in your first financial transactions, such as withdrawing cash, making a purchase with your debit card, or transferring funds, it feels like using a brand-new tool for the first time. Remember that each transaction, each swipe, and each click shape your financial future.

Step 7: Keep Growing Your Treasure

Finally, make it a ritual to regularly review and manage your account. Regularly pausing to use your financial tools, standing back, and evaluating your handiwork can be seen as a way to review and manage your account. Regularly checking your account balance, tracking your expenses, and setting savings goals are acts of devotion to your financial well-being. These habits will help you grow a healthy relationship with money and guide you toward financial maturity and independence.

DIGITAL VAULTS: ONLINE AND MOBILE BANKING

Welcome to the digital era of banking, where the grand vaults of finance extend beyond the towering walls of physical banks into the vast, interconnected world of the internet. Users can access online and mobile banking from anywhere, exploring hidden chambers within these vaults that are filled with tools and treasures. But navigating these chambers requires not just knowledge but also caution, as the digital realm is vast and sometimes fraught with invisible risks.

Tips for Safe Navigation

- **Create strong, unique passwords**: Your password is like the secret key to your personal treasure chest. Make sure it is strong (a mix of letters, numbers, and symbols) and unique (not used for any other accounts). A strong password is like a complex lock that keeps intruders out.
- **Beware of phishing expeditions**: Just as pirates used to trick sailors, modern cyber pirates use phishing scams to trick you into giving away your personal information. Be vigilant! Never click on suspicious links or give out your banking details in response to unsolicited emails or messages.
- **Use secure networks**: Accessing your online banking on public Wi-Fi is like counting your gold in a crowded marketplace. Always use a secure, private internet connection to protect your information from prying eyes.
- **Enable two-factor authentication (2FA)**: This is like having an extra guard at the door of our vault. 2FA adds an additional layer of security by requiring a second form of verification (like a text message code) to access your account.

- **Regularly check your accounts**: Regularly logging in to check your accounts is like making frequent visits to your vault to ensure all your treasures are safe. It helps you spot any unusual activity early.
- **Update your banking apps**: Keeping your banking up-to-date is like reinforcing the walls of your vault. Updates often include security enhancements that protect your data from new threats.
- **Download banking apps only from trusted sources**: Only download banking apps from official app stores or your bank's website. Downloading apps from unverified sources is like picking up a mysterious map that could lead to a trap.
- **Log out after each session**: Always log out of your banking app or website when you are done, closing the vault door firmly behind you. This prevents anyone else from accessing your account if our device falls into the wrong hands.
- **Educate yourself on online banking features**: Make sure you understand the features and settings of your online banking platform. Knowing how to navigate your digital banking tools is like understanding the layout of a complex treasure map.
- **Contact your bank immediately if you suspect anything is wrong**: If you notice anything unusual, contact your bank immediately. It is like alerting the guards that something might be wrong in the vault.

GUARDIANS OF YOUR WEALTH: THE ROLE OF BANKS

Imagine a grand medieval castle with towering walls and a deep moat, standing resiliently in the face of threats and time. Banks act as guardians of your financial well-being, ensuring that your treasure is safely tucked inside. They play a crucial role in safeguarding and nurturing your wealth.

Safeguarding Deposits: The Castle's Strongest Vault

The first and foremost role of these guardians is to safeguard your deposits. Imagine each deposit you make as a precious gemstone, and the bank as a castle with the strongest vault. Government insurance, like the FDIC in the U.S., ensures that your treasure is protected even if the castle faces unforeseen calamities, providing security beyond just physical measures.

Providing Loans: The Magical Forge

At banks, dreams are transformed into reality through their magical forging power. The bank delves into its vaults and lends you the gold you may need—anything from a car to a college education to a dream vacation—when you seek a loan. You need to give back the money they lend you with extra (the interest). Stay away from loans unless absolutely necessary!

Facilitating Payments: The Messenger Network

Messengers in medieval times carried messages across vast distances to facilitate trade and commerce. In the modern world, this is like banks managing transactions. Whether it is a check, a direct deposit, or an electronic transfer, banks ensure your money reaches its destination swiftly and safely, like a well-escorted caravan traveling through a kingdom.

Choosing Your Guardian: Selecting the Right Bank

As you start on this journey, choosing the right guardian—your bank—is as crucial as a knight choosing a loyal squire. This choice can shape your path, offering support and the tools needed for your quest.

- **Interest rates**: Look for a bank that offers competitive interest rates, both for savings and loans. This rate determines how much your savings will grow and how much borrowing will cost you.
- **Online vs. brick-and-mortar**: Decide between a traditional brick-and-mortar bank and an online bank. While traditional banks offer in-person services, online banks often offer higher interest rates and lower fees, thanks to their lower overhead costs.
- **Customer service**: Look at the bank's customer service. Responsive and helpful customer service is like a squire who is always ready to assist his master, ensuring a smooth journey and promptly addressing challenges.
- **Online features**: In today's digital age, having a bank with robust online features is like having a map that shows not only the paths but also the shortcuts. Easy access to online banking, mobile apps, and digital payment options can make managing your finances more convenient.
- **Fees and minimums**: Be wary of the dragons of the banking world—fees and minimum balance requirements. Some banks charge for account maintenance, ATM usage, or have a minimum balance requirement. Choose a bank where the fees are minimal or fit with your banking habits.

Banks are not just financial institutions; they are guardians and facilitators on your journey towards financial maturity. As you choose your guardian, consider these factors carefully, ensuring that your chosen bank aligns with your needs, goals, and the path you wish to tread in your financial adventure. With the right guardian by your side, the treasures of stability, growth, and opportunity await you in the grand adventure of your financial life.

Imagine standing at the edge of a vast, unknown forest—the Forest of Unforeseen Circumstances. How do you traverse such a landscape with confidence and security? This is where the concepts of emergency funds and insurance come in handy; they can serve as a shield and compass in this treacherous terrain. So, join us in the next chapter, where we will light a torch to guide you through these shadows, unraveling the mysteries of emergency funds and insurance and empowering you with the knowledge to traverse this terrain with confidence and foresight.

4

SAFE HAVENS

In a world rife with financial pitfalls, how do you build your financial fortress? A fortress that stands resilient against the sudden storms of life's unpredictability. In this chapter, "Safe Havens," we lay the bricks of such a fortress—emergency funds and insurance. The scary thing is that 57% of people in the U.S. say that they know they don't have enough money in their emergency account (Gillespie, 2023). Fortunately, you can avoid being part of this statistic by taking action today and preparing for future challenges.

Imagine a medieval kingdom where each family builds their own stronghold to protect against unforeseen invasions and calamities. In our modern financial kingdom, the unexpected can take many forms: a sudden job loss, a medical emergency, or the theft of valuables. These are the invaders of our financial peace. And yet, startlingly, over half of the population finds themselves unprepared for such sieges (McNair, 2023).

Recent statistics paint a sobering picture: A survey by Bankrate revealed that only 40% of Americans could cover an unexpected

$1,000 expense with their savings (Green, 2023). This worrying figure underscores a widespread vulnerability in a kingdom where many fortresses remain alarmingly unfortified. Furthermore, the Federal Reserve reports that nearly 25% of adults have no retirement savings or pension, highlighting a lack of long-term financial armor (USAFactsTeam, 2023).

Don't become a statistic! Instead, let this chapter be your guide to constructing a robust financial defense. We will delve into the essentials of emergency funds: how much to save, where to keep it, and how to build it, even when it seems like a daunting task. Then we will navigate the complex world of insurance, understanding how it acts as a shield, protecting you against the financial impacts of life's major events. By the end of this chapter, you will have the understanding and tools to start building your financial fortress, brick by brick. A fortress that not only guards against immediate financial threats but also lays the foundation for a secure and prosperous financial future.

PREPARING FOR RAINY DAYS: YOUR EMERGENCY FUND

In the mythical kingdom of your finances, emergency funds are like magical force fields, shimmering around your kingdom, guarding it against the unexpected storms that life might hurl your way. Your emergency fund is not just a buffer; it serves as a powerful shield charged with the magic of foresight and preparation.

The Foundation Stone: How Much to Save

The first stone in your protective wall is deciding how much to save. A common strategy is to gather enough gold to cover three to six months of living expenses. But remember, as your circumstances change, you need to change the amount you have available as well.

The Vault of Safekeeping: Where to Keep Your Money

Choosing where to keep your emergency fund is like selecting the safest vault in the castle. Your funds need to be easily accessible but also secure. High-yield savings accounts, or money market accounts, are typically the best accounts to use, as they offer a balance of accessibility, safety, and above-average interest rates.

Let's Get Practical

As we conclude our journey through the magical world of emergency funds, let us take action to build our protective force field. Each step in building your emergency fund is another layer of added strength. Let's explore these crucial steps:

- **Set your savings goals**: Start with a clear savings goal. This is like choosing the perimeter of protection. Determine the total amount you want to save based on your monthly budget, and set this as your target.
- **Automatic transfers**: Introduce a power source—automatic transfers. Set up a monthly transfer from your checking account to your emergency fund. This step is like adding fuel that continuously powers the field, reinforcing your shield's strength over time without needing constant attention.
- **Budget Adjustments**: Calibrate your energy levels. Review your budget to find areas where you can cut back. Each dollar saved will boost shield durability gradually but significantly.

- **Extra income**: Occasionally, you may find rare materials that provide a surge of power. You can receive this money through extra income sources such as a part-time job or as a gift.
- **Avoid unnecessary withdrawals**: Once it's up and running, it is crucial to preserve your force field's integrity. Avoid dipping into your emergency fund for non-essential expenses. This step is like adding a preservative to make sure your barrier retains its power.

By following these steps, you build a resilient force field around your financial kingdom—your emergency fund—that protects your financial well-being. An emergency fund will serve as a bulwark against life's unexpected challenges, keeping your financial kingdom secure and thriving.

ARMOR AND SHIELDS: THE MULTIFACETED WORLD OF INSURANCE

In the grand theater of life's epic battles, insurance stands as the vital armor that warriors wear to ensure their survival and resilience. Far from being mere financial products, these diverse forms of insurance are guardians, each playing a critical role in protecting different facets of our lives. While you may still be covered by your parent's insurance, now is the time to prepare for the day you need to go at it on your own. Did you know you need your own health insurance after age 25 (Internal Revenue Service, 2023)? In this chapter, we will guide you through the different types of insurance so you can be well-informed when the time comes to manage them yourself.

Health Insurance

Health insurance covers medical expenses and offers protection against the high costs of healthcare. It ensures that a health crisis does not morph into a financial catastrophe.

Auto Insurance

From minor dents to major collisions, auto insurance shields us from potentially crippling financial impacts.

Life Insurance

In the event of your death, it provides financial support to loved ones left behind.

Homeowners or Renters Insurance

It safeguards your home and belongings from perils like fire, theft, and natural disasters.

Disability Insurance

This type of insurance provides financial support in the event of an inability to work due to injury or illness.

Liability Insurance

Whether it is a mistake or an unforeseen event that leads to legal claims against you, this insurance provides counsel and resources to navigate turbulent waters.

Each type of insurance serves as a guardian in various arenas of life. They are not just contracts; they are commitments to protect your financial well-being against the uncertainties of life's journey. Understanding and choosing the right insurance is an important step in fortifying yourself against the myriad of challenges that lie ahead in the great adventure of life!

As we conclude this section, let's look at how to choose the right insurance plan for your needs:

- **Understand the risks**: Are you a frequent traveler, a homeowner, a car owner, or the primary earner in your family? Your lifestyle will determine the type of insurance you need.
- **Know your enemy**: Evaluate the potential risks you may face. For health insurance, think of your health history. For auto insurance, think about the type of car you drive and your driving habits. For life insurance, think of your financial obligations (like debt and dependents).
- **Choose your armor wisely**: Not all insurance policies are created equal. Look for policies that offer comprehensive coverage for your specific needs. Don't just look at the premiums; also look at the coverage limits, deductibles, and exclusions.
- **Read the small print**: Insurance policies can be complex. Read the terms carefully. Carefully understand the fine print, including what is covered, what is not, and how to file a claim. Discuss with your parents.
- **Compare**: Shop around and compare different policies. Just as a warrior would test different swords, you should compare the features, costs, and benefits of various insurance plans.

- **Seek advice**: if you are unsure, seek advice from financial advisors or insurance experts. They can help you navigate the complex world of insurance and choose the right protection for your specific needs.
- **Regularly sharpen your sword**: Review your insurance needs regularly. As your life changes—say, you buy a new car or start a new job—your insurance needs might change too.

By following these steps, you can confidently choose the right insurance plan and be sure that you are well-equipped for the various duels and quests that life presents. This process, though it may be a bit complex, is empowering, arming you with the knowledge and protection you need to journey forth with confidence in your grand financial adventure.

As we draw the curtains on this chapter of armor and shields, we have fortified your immediate defenses against the unforeseen skirmishes of life. But now, a new horizon beckons. Are you ready to embark on the grand feat of constructing a towering citadel, one that will secure your future? The expansive realm of savings lies beyond the walls of immediate protection, where wealth is not just guarded but grown. A fortress of financial strength and stability awaits your mastery. Prepare to delve into the art of building your savings—the ultimate bastion of your financial future.

5

THE SAVINGS CITADEL

What if I told you that the secret to lasting wealth isn't making more money but keeping more of what you make? Welcome to the savings citadel—your fortress for the future.

UNDERSTAND THE IMPORTANCE OF SAVING MONEY

As we start on the journey of *The Savings Citadel*, imagine the act of saving as the grand endeavor of building a castle. Each coin you save is not merely a stone laid but a strategic step in fortifying your financial future. This castle represents more than just a hoard of wealth; it is a symbol of your foresight, discipline, and commitment to a future where you stand resilient and secure. Each saved coin, a testament to your hard work, gradually forms the walls, towers, and ramparts of your fortress, shielding you from future uncertainties and helping you to see instead a future filled with possibilities and dreams.

Let's raise banners high on the ramparts, each one fluttering with a different motivation for saving. These banners symbolize your life goals and dreams, guiding you in your journey toward financial mastery.

Financial Independence

This banner flies with the symbol of freedom. Financial independence means having enough savings to live on without relying on your parents and, ultimately, not relying on a job either. It is about having the freedom to live your life as you please, free from financial restrictions. Saving towards this goal empowers you to live life on your terms.

Emergency Funds

The banner of security and readiness. Having an emergency fund means you are prepared for life's unexpected turns. It is your financial safety net, ensuring that when life throws curveballs at you, you are ready to catch them without toppling over.

Debt-Free Living

Saving to pay off debts is about freeing yourself from the chains of financial obligations by living beneath your means. Imagine life without the weight of debt; it is lighter, isn't it? Each coin saved takes you a step closer to this liberating goal.

Better Retirement

This banner waves with the promise of a comfortable and secure future. Saving for retirement is about ensuring that your golden years are just that—golden. It is about picturing your future self and thanking you for the comfortable lifestyle you have ensured for them.

Achieve Long-Term Financial Goals

This banner is adorned with your dreams, be it owning a home, going to college, or traveling the world. Long-term financial goals require patience and consistent saving, but the reward is living out your dreams.

Investing

The banner of growth and opportunity. Saving to invest is about putting your money to work for you. It is about growing your wealth through strategic investments, turning your savings into a seedbed for financial gains.

Planning for expenses

The banner of practicality and planning. Expenses like annual insurance premiums or semester tuition fees are expected, but they don't come every month. By saving for these expenses, you can avoid being caught off-guard when they arrive.

Job Loss

The banner of resilience. In an uncertain job market, having savings can mean the difference between panic and peace during periods of unemployment. It gives you the time and space to find a new job without the pressure of immediate financial distress.

Living the Good Life

The banner of wellbeing. Saving is not just about the tangible goals; it is also about the intangible sense of well-being. Knowing you are financially responsible and secure can significantly reduce your stress and increase your overall happiness and quality of life.

Just as the foundations of a castle are crucial to the stability of its walls and towers, savings are the foundations of any financial blueprint. Just as the bedrock supports the construction of a castle, savings support the building of your financial kingdom. Without strong foundations, even the grandest castle can crumble. Similarly, without a solid base of savings, your financial plans, no matter how well-structured, may not withstand the challenges of time. So, prioritize building and strengthening your savings. It is the groundwork that supports all your future financial endeavors, enabling you to build a life that is not just rich in wealth but also in choices, opportunities, and security.

THE TREASURY ROOM: SMART TIPS FOR EFFECTIVE SAVING

In the heart of your savings citadel lies the Treasury Room, a spectacular chamber filled with golden coins, sparkling jewels, and valuable treasures. But accumulating wealth is not just about stashing away your money; it is also about planning, smart strategies, and consistent effort. With the right tips and techniques for effective saving, you can gradually fill your treasury, making sure it glows with the riches of financial well-being and security.

Let's look at some strategies to transform your ordinary income into a growing treasure:

Paying Oneself First: The Alchemy of Transformation

Treat your savings as if they were the Philosopher's Stone, a source of untold potential. Whenever income flows your way, the first act of alchemy to perform is to turn a portion of that into your savings. This is the powerful practice of adding to your savings first before paying anything else. By implementing this practice, you can effectively turn something ordinary into something remarkable for your future.

Mastering the Realm of Finance: Your Kingdom's Strategy

Think of budgeting as strategic planning for running your own kingdom. It is about mapping out your empire of income and expenses and wisely allocating resources to different sectors like needs, wants, and savings. Just as a wise ruler balances immediate needs with the future prosperity of their kingdom, effective budgeting ensures a harmonious balance between your current lifestyle and future financial goals. It is all about making smart strategic decisions that shape it.

The Magic of Compound Interest: The Sorcerer's Multiplier

Compound interest is one of the most powerful tools in your savings citadel. Compound interest allows your savings to grow not only from your contributions but also from the interest earned over time. It is like real-life magic that multiplies your gold, turning small savings into a substantial hoard over the years.

Here is how it works: When you save money in an account that earns interest, you don't just earn interest on the original amount but also on the interest that accumulates over time. It is like planting a magical seed. The initial interest is like the first sprout, which then grows and sprouts its own leaves. As time goes on, those leaves (the interest) grow and sprout more leaves (more interest). So, with compound interest, your money tree doesn't just grow; it flourishes wildly, far beyond the size of the original seed. This is why starting to save early can lead to much larger treasure in your treasury room, as the magic of compound interest has more time to work its spell.

Magical Automation: The Invisible Hand of Savings

Set up automatic transfers to your savings account. This invisible hand quietly and consistently moves money into your savings, building your treasure without you lifting a finger.

The Potion of Frugality: The Elixir of Preservation

Practice frugality. Cut unnecessary expenses and be mindful of your spending. Each coin you save adds to your treasury. It is not about deprivation but about smart management of resources. Here are some practical tips for being frugal:

- **Track your spending**: Keep a log of your expenses. Understanding where your money goes is like having a map of your financial landscape.
- **Budget wisely**: Allocate funds for necessities first, then savings, followed by wants. This ensures you are covering all bases while still contributing to your treasury.
- **Shop smart**: Look for deals, use coupons, and compare prices. It is like hunting for the most valuable ingredients at the best price.
- **DIY magic**: Embrace the do-it-yourself spirit. Whether it is cooking at home or repairing things yourself, each act adds to your potion.
- **Limit eating out**: While dining out is convenient, it is often more expensive. Eating at home can be both a delightful adventure and a way to save.
- **Mindful entertainment**: Seek free or low-cost entertainment options. Parks, libraries, and community events are treasure troves of enjoyment without a heavy cost.
- **Second-hand treasures**: Buying second-hand items or swapping with friends can be both fun and frugal.

The Shield Against Impulse: The Barrier Spell

Create a shield against impulse buying. Wait for a set period before making large purchases. This barrier spell provides you with the opportunity to assess whether the purchase is necessary or if the money would be better saved for your treasury. Here is how you can strengthen this shield:

- **Wait it out**: If you still feel it is necessary after a week or two, it is likely a worthwhile buy.
- **Question your motives**: Ask yourself why you want to make the purchase. Is it a need or a want? Understanding the motive behind your spending can help curb impulsive purchases.
- **Budget for treats**: Allocate a small portion of your budget for 'fun money'. This allows you to indulge occasionally without breaking the bank.
- **Avoid temptation**: Unsubscribe from marketing emails, and avoid browsing online stores or malls without a specific purpose.
- **The power of lists**: Stick to a shopping list when you go out. It is like a magical scroll that keeps you focused on what you truly need.

Now that you have ventured through the corridors of wisdom and uncovered the secrets of effective saving, it is time to start filling your treasury room! Think of this as an invitation to join an elite guild of smart savers, a group of wise financial wizards who understand the art of growing wealth. By embracing these strategies, you are not just saving money; you are unlocking a secret level in the game of life, a level where financial stability and freedom await. Begin your journey today. Every coin saved is a step closer to achieving your dreams and securing your future. Welcome to the guild; your treasure awaits!

THE FUTURE'S HORIZON: HOW SAVINGS ILLUMINATE YOUR PATH FORWARD

Imagine standing atop the citadel you have built, gazing out over a vast kingdom of endless possibilities. Your diligent savings have made this breathtaking view, with horizons stretching far and wide, possible. Your diligent savings, with each coin saved, built this towering structure, elevating you to see and dream bigger. It is a testament to your discipline and foresight, a reminder that your financial goals and aspirations are within reach. From this vantage point, you can explore a future that is not just a distant dream but a landscape of opportunities.

Having a solid savings account is like having a magic key to new adventures. Think of it as your ticket to explore new lands and undertake epic quests, or just chill with the cool options it brings. With enough saved up, you can think about things like starting your own YouTube channel, going on a road trip with friends, or maybe even starting a small online business. It is not just about having cash in the bank; it is about the freedom and choices that cash gives you. You can dream big, take chances, or just enjoy the peace of mind knowing you have a financial cushion to fall back on. In the world of savings, more coins means more choices, and who doesn't love having options?

While your citadel stands tall, maintaining its grandeur in a world teeming with tempting expenditures and siren calls to spend is the next challenge. In the next pillar, *Tactical Budgeting and Spending*, we will navigate through the art of smart spending without compromising the integrity of your savings fortress. Get ready to arm yourself with strategies that balance enjoying the present while securing your future. This chapter is your guide to being a savvy spender and making sure your financial citadel remains unassailable.

PILLAR 3

TACTICAL BUDGETING AND SPENDING

Budgeting has only one rule: Do not go over budget.

— LESLIE TAYNE

6

BUDGETING BOOTCAMP

What if you could easily navigate the battlefield of life with a financial compass? This chapter delves into the essential skill of budgeting, which is far more than just counting pennies. It is about crafting your financial destiny. Through budgeting, you gain a clear understanding of where your money goes, empowering you to make informed decisions that fit in with your goals and values. By mastering the art of budgeting, you are not just organizing your finances; you are charting a course toward your desired future. This chapter is your guide to turning budgeting from a mundane task into a powerful tool for building the life you want.

BOOT CAMP BASICS: THE UNBREAKABLE ARMOR OF BUDGETING

Imagine you are at the starting line of an adrenaline-pumping boot camp. Ahead lies a challenging obstacle course, with each hurdle and barrier designed to test your endurance, skill, and determination. There is a drill sergeant shouting instructions, pushing you to the limit, forcing you to dig deep and find strength you didn't know you had. Imagine this intense, exhilarating scenario about budgeting. Yes, budgeting! Budgeting is the ultimate form of financial training, a rigorous course that strengthens your money management muscles. Each challenge in this budgeting boot camp teaches you to navigate your finances with precision and confidence, turning you into a master of your monitoring destiny.

Budgeting, in the most practical sense, is like mapping out your financial journey. It is about knowing exactly how much gold you have in your coffers (income) and how much you need to spend on your army's provisions (expenses). Think of budgeting as crafting magical armor. It is the armor that shields you from the unexpected arrows of financial calamity, like sudden expenses or economic downturns. At the same time, it is your carefully designed battle plan, guiding you to conquer your financial goals, be they saving for a new gadget, going to college, or just having enough to enjoy outings with friends. This armor and strategy combined make you not just a participant in the financial world but a confident commander of your own economic destiny.

Budgeting 101

A basic budget is like your financial game plan. It is like keeping score in a video game, but instead of points, you are tracking your money. Here is how it works:

- **Income**: This is your "score"—the money you earn or receive, like a part-time job, an allowance, or birthday money.
- **Expenses**: These are the things you spend money on. Think of them as in-game purchases. This can be stuff like your phone bill, snacks, or movie tickets.

- **Savings**: This is like setting aside extra lives for future levels. It is part of your money you don't spend but save for later, maybe for something like a new phone or college.
- **Balance**: This is what is left after you subtract your expenses and savings from your income. It is like your final score after a gaming session.

The goal is to make sure your "score" (income) is always enough to cover your "purchases" (expenses) and have some left for "extra lives" (savings).

Budgeting is not merely counting pennies; think of it as sculpting your future in monetary marble. It is a work of art that requires both discipline and strategy. With a well-planned budget, you are not just tracking expenses; you are chiseling away at your dreams and goals, giving them shape in the real world. Without budgeting, those dreams might remain elusive, like uncarved marble blocks.

Steps for Budgeting

1. **Track Your Income**: Write all sources of income down.
2. **List our expenses**: Include both fixed (like subscriptions) and variable (like eating out).
3. **Set savings goals**: Decide on a percentage or amount to save.
4. **Allocate funds wisely**: Divide your income between needs, wants, and savings.
5. **Monitor regularly**: Regularly monitor your spending and make adjustments as necessary.

Here is an example of what you would find in a budget:

Category	Amount
Income	
Part-time job	$300
Allowance	$50
Total Income	**$350**
Expenses	
Savings (20% of income)	$70
Phone bill	$40
Transportation	$30
Entertainment (movies, games)	$50
Eating out	$40
Clothing	$30
Miscellaneous (gifts, etc)	$20
Total expenses	**$280**
Remaining balance	**$70**

Keep in mind that each budget decision you make has a lasting impact on your financial future. Plan wisely!

TOOLS OF THE TRADE: YOUR BUDGETING ARSENAL

Starting the budgeting process is like assembling an armory of weapons for a skilled warrior. Just as a warrior needs the right tools for battle, you need the right tools for managing your finances. Each tool in your budgeting arsenal serves a specific purpose, helping you to plan, track, and control your spending and savings. With this toolkit, you strategically plan and execute your financial moves, ensuring that every dollar is used in the best possible way to secure your financial future.

On the financial battlefield, various budgeting worksheets and apps are like specialized pieces of equipment, each designed for unique scenarios:

Mint

Think of Mint as your reconnaissance drone, providing an overview of your entire financial landscape. Connect all your financial accounts to see them all in one place. It tracks your spending, creates budgets, and even monitors your credit score.

You Need a Budget (YNAB)

This is like a precision-guided weapon, ideal for those who need to get a very detailed and disciplined grip on their finances. It is great for allocating every dollar to a job and tracking your goals.

PocketGuard

Like a lightweight shield, PocketGuard simplifies budgeting by showing how much money you have after spending money, and after setting aside funds for bills, goals, and necessities.

Each of these tools offers unique features to help you manage your money effectively, like a well-equipped warrior ready for any financial challenge.

In wrapping up this section on budgeting, remember that a budget is your financial compass, guiding you through the twists and turns of economic life. Start by tracking your income and expenses, then set realistic goals for saving and spending. Be adaptable; your budget is a living plan that can change as your life does. Most importantly, be consistent and disciplined with your budgeting practice. Over time, these habits will build a strong financial foundation, turning budgeting from a chore into a powerful tool for achieving your dreams and securing your future.

Remember, the art of budgeting is the art of mastering your money.

THE STRATEGY ROOM: BUDGETING FOR BIG-TICKET BATTLEGROUNDS

Throughout history, legendary battles and colossal campaigns have been won not only through might but also through careful planning and strategy. Think of Alexander the Great's conquests or the strategic brilliance of the Battle of Normandy. Each of these monumental events required detailed planning and foresight. And when it comes to managing your finances, planning for a big purchase is akin to preparing for a grand campaign. Whether it's a car, a college fund, or a significant tech gadget, these big-ticket items are your financial battlegrounds. Grand endeavors require grand plans—a budget that meticulously maps out your path to victory, ensuring that your financial conquests are as triumphant as those legendary campaigns of old.

Financial Goals and Budgeting

Setting financial goals is a crucial prelude to effective budgeting. It is about turning your dreams and life goals into achievable financial targets. Whether you dream of buying a car, vacationing in the Bahamas, or securing a comfortable retirement, it all starts with setting clear financial goals.

Short-term goals (1–2 years)

These often involve smaller, more tangible purchases or savings objectives. Examples include saving for a new smartphone, funding a summer trip, buying concert tickets, or even putting aside money for holiday gifts. Here are some tips for saving towards a short-term goal:

- **Be specific**: Know exactly what you are saving for, like a specific model of a phone or a trip to a particular place.
- **Set a deadline**: Have a time by which you want to reach your goal; for example, you want to buy a new laptop by the summer.
- **Create a savings plan**: Break down the total amount into manageable monthly or weekly savings.
- **Stay disciplined**: Stick to your savings plan by cutting unnecessary expenses or finding ways to increase your income.
- **Track progress**: Regularly check your savings to ensure you are on track to meet your goal.

Mid-term Goals (3–5 years)

These often involve saving for larger, more significant expenditures or life events. These might include putting a down payment on a car, saving for a special international trip, funding a significant home renovation, or starting a college fund. To effectively achieve mid-term goals:

- **Assess and prioritize**: Understand what is most important to you in the next few years and focus on that.
- **Calculate the cost**: Estimate the total amount needed for your goal.
- **Formulate a savings strategy**: Create a plan that allocates a portion of your income towards these goals regularly.
- **Consider investment**: For goals that are four to five years away, you might consider low-risk investments to grow your savings faster.
- **Review regularly**: Mid-term goals often need periodic reassessment to align with changes in our income, expenses, or priorities.

Long-term Goals (5+ years and beyond)

These are your big-picture dreams, like buying a house or saving for retirement (you are never too young to start!). They demand a long-term commitment and often involve investing in growing your savings.

You may set a goal that requires you to make a large purchase; good for you! This can be both scary and exciting. To be successful in making a big expenditure, like a car or a big vacation, here are some steps you can follow to make it less stressful:

Reconnaissance (Research)

Understanding the enemy (the market): Just like a general survey of the battlefield, you need to research the market. Here is how you can approach this phase:

- **Define your needs and wants**: For a car, consider price, size, fuel efficiency, and other features that may be important to you. For a vacation, think about how you will get there (fly or drive), the cost of food, and the specific amenities (like a pool or beach) you want.
- **Compare and research prices**: Use online platforms to get an idea of the going rates for cars or homes in your desired area.
- **Cost of ownership**: For a car, think about things like insurance, maintenance, and the cost of fuel. For a vacation, consider trip insurance, excursions, and food.
- **Additional costs**: Don't forget additional costs like registration fees for a car or currency exchange for a vacation.

Resource Allocation (Savings)

This is where you build your war chest. Determine how much money you need for the payment and additional costs.

- **Set a clear savings goal**: Based on your research, set a realistic savings target for your down payment and other associated costs.
- **Create a savings plan**: Break down your goal into monthly or weekly savings targets. This helps make the goal more manageable.
- **Cut back on non-essentials**: Temporarily reduce spending on non-essential items to boost your savings rate.
- **Consider high-interest savings accounts**: Place your savings in an account that earns more interest to help your money grow faster.
- **Track your progress**: Regularly monitor your savings to stay motivated and make adjustments if needed.

A note of caution on borrowing and debt is crucial. As young readers of this book, our strongest recommendation is to save cash for your purchases. However, we understand that sometimes life throws unexpected challenges, and taking on debt becomes necessary. The following steps will equip you with the knowledge to navigate this terrain cautiously. If you are not going to borrow money, jump straight to the last step: The Conquest!

Formation of Allies (Building Credit)

In this phase, you are building your army—your credit score. It is important when securing loans with better interest rates. Here is how to build your credit score:

- **Start early**: If you are under age 18, your parents can help you build credit by simply contacting their credit card issuer and asking them to add you to their account as an Authorized User. Tell your parent that this will let you begin to build a credit history based on their spending and suggest that they keep the credit card issued in your name in their possession so it will never be used. Win-win since your parent can help you build credit, and neither of you has to worry about using the new credit card.
- **Use credit wisely**: Once you have a credit card, use it responsibly. Keep balances low and pay off the full amount each month.
- **Pay bills on time**: Late payments can hurt your credit score. Set reminders or auto-pay to stay on track.
- **Monitor your credit**: Regularly check your credit report for errors and understand how different actions affect your score.
- **Limit new credit applications**: Too many applications can negatively impact your credit score.

Siege Weapons (Loan Pre-Approval)

But here is a word of caution before you wield your weapon: use loans wisely. Every dollar you pay in interest is a dollar you could have been saving! It is best to use loans only for big purchases like a house or car; use cash for smaller purchases.

If you have decided to borrow money, you need to siege weapons and get pre-approved for a loan. This shows the seller you are serious and ready to battle. Here is how to wield this weapon:

- **Involve a guardian**: If you are under 18, you will need a parent or guardian to co-sign any loan, as minors can't legally enter into a contract.

- **Understand pre-approval**: Loan pre-approval gives you an idea of how much you can borrow and signals to sellers that you are a serious buyer.
- **Gather the necessary documents**: You might need to provide proof of income (if you have a job), bank statements and other financial documents.
- **Stay within budget**: Just because you are pre-approved for a certain amount doesn't mean you should max it out. Stick to what you can comfortably afford.

The Skirmishes (Negotiations)

This is like engaging in tactical battles before a final victory.

- **Involve an adult**: Teens should involve a parent or guardian in negotiations, especially since legal contracts require an adult's involvement.
- **Do your homework**: Know the value of what you are buying, like the market price of the car or home.
- **Stay firm but fair**: Understand your budget limits and don't be afraid to negotiate for a better deal, but also be reasonable.
- **Be prepared to walk away**: If the deal doesn't meet your criteria or feels off, be ready to look elsewhere.

The Conquest (Purchase)

This is the high point of the long-term goal journey. Let's see what you need to do and keep in mind:

- **Final review with an adult**: Go over the details of the purchase and the financial implications with a parent or guardian.

- **Understand the contract**: Before signing any documents, make sure you (and your guardian) fully understand all the terms and conditions.
- **Seal the deal**: Once everything checks out, finalize the purchase. Whether it is signing for a car or making a down payment on a major item, this is where your planning and hard work pay off.
- **Celebrate responsibly**: Acknowledge this major achievement, but also remember the responsibility that comes with it.

In the world of finance, remember that the one with a well-crafted plan holds the power. Budgeting for big purchases isn't just a practical task; it is a high-stakes strategy in the art of financial warfare. By meticulously planning, researching, and saving, you are not just buying something; you are strategically conquering financial goals. So, wield your budgeting skills like a master strategist, and you will be well on your way to winning financial wars.

Congratulations! You've survived *Budgeting Bootcamp* and emerged with new armor and a war chest of tools. But what if the battlefield is merely an illusion—a tempting mirage crafted to lure you away from your carefully crafted plans?

7

THE MIRAGE OF CONSUMERISM

With every corner shouting "Buy this!" in today's world, it is easy to get swept up in a spending spree. Did you know that, on average, teens spend about $2,250 a year? (Lexington Law, 2019) That is a lot of cash! So, how do we sift through the endless barrage of ads and offers, separating genuine needs from mere wants? It is time to pull back the curtain on the illusions of consumerism. By understanding the tricks of the trade and being mindful of our spending habits, we can make smarter, more informed decisions about where our money goes. Let's dive in and unravel these mysteries.

MIRAGE MASTERS: DECIPHERING THE ILLUSION OF NEEDS VS. WANTS

Picture this: You are wandering through a vast, sun-scorched desert, your throat parched, and your legs weary. Suddenly, up ahead, you spot a shimmering oasis with water sparkling and palm trees swaying. When you get close to it, you realize that it is just a mirage that the heat has created. This is exactly what consumerism does to us. It creates enticing illusions of happiness and fulfillment through endless buying and accumulating stuff. But, just like the desert mirage, these promises are empty. As a teen, you are at a stage where understanding this message is crucial. Getting caught up in the hype of the latest trends or gadgets and feeling like owning them is the key to happiness or popularity is easy. But the truth is, genuine contentment often lies beyond the endless cycle of buying. In this chapter, we will explore the "mirage of consumerism" and learn how to spot and avoid these illusions, focusing on what truly matters for long-lasting happiness and fulfillment.

Deciphering the tricky and often deceptive line between what we need and what we want, social media platforms like TikTok and Instagram further blur this line as influencers and companies spend billions to create enticing illusions of lifestyles and products. According to Barysevich (2020), 70% of people admit that they are more inclined to purchase items that receive positive reviews or referrals on social media platforms. These platforms can make it seem like everyone has the latest gadgets, trendiest clothes, or ideal lifestyles, pressuring us to want these things too. You need to constantly remind yourself that you may be seeing a mirage. For example, despite the lavish lifestyles often portrayed, most Americans don't have $5,000 in savings, highlighting the gap between the illusion and reality (Payne, 2023a). In this chapter, we want to show you how to see through these illusions, helping you make smarter, more realistic financial decisions.

Navigating the Desert of Needs and Wants

Understanding the difference between needs and wants is crucial to mastering your finances.

Needs are essentials—the things you cannot live without—like food, shelter, basic clothing, and healthcare. For instance, you need a smartphone for school or work, but do you need the latest model with all the bells and whistles? Probably not.

Wants, on the other hand, are items or experiences we desire but don't necessarily need for survival. That latest gaming console or designer jacket? They are cool, sure, but they are wants, not needs.

Imagine you are scrolling through Instagram or TikTok. You observe influencers sporting expensive devices, fashionable clothing, and what appears to be an endless supply of cool stuff. It is easy to start thinking you need these things to fit in or feel happy. But here's the catch: these platforms are often a stage for advertising. Companies and influencers are really good at making their products seem essential, but remember, they are trying to sell you something. Let's say you have saved $500. You are eyeing a new gaming console that costs exactly that much. It is tempting, right? But pause for a minute. Do you have enough saved for college textbooks or that school trip next month? Those are needs. The gaming console is a want.

Balancing needs and wants is about making choices. You can still buy cool stuff, but it is about timing and priority. Maybe set a smaller savings goal for the console while keeping the majority of your savings for more essential things. Remember, falling for the "wants" mirage can lead to financial stress.

In closing this section, remember that learning to distinguish between needs and wants is like having x-ray vision to see through illusions. Developing this superpower enables you to see through tricky marketing and avoid being deceived by the false lives others portray on social media. By mastering this, you become not just a savvy spender but a wise navigator, able to steer through the mirage-laden desert of modern consumerism with clarity and purpose. This skill will serve as a vital tool in your journey toward financial independence and security.

THE OASIS OF DELAYED GRATIFICATION: PATIENCE AS YOUR SECRET WEAPON

In the timeless fable of *The Hare and the Tortoise*, the swift hare boasts of his speed, mocking the slow-moving tortoise. However, overconfident in his quickness, the hare takes a nap mid-race, while the tortoise, steady and determined, ultimately wins. This story is a perfect metaphor for patience over impulsivity, especially if we look at spending. Just like the hare, it is tempting to rush into purchases for instant gratification. However, embracing the tortoise's patience, saving steadily, and thinking long-term can lead to greater gratification and life fulfillment. It is about pacing your financial journey and understanding that sometimes, slow and steady wins the race.

Ready to become a pro at waiting for the good stuff in life? We have some cool exercises to train you in the art of delaying gratification. Think of it as training for your financial fitness, like how a superhero hones their skills. These challenges are not just about holding off on spending; they are about building up your patience muscles for bigger, better rewards down the line. So, gear up for an exciting journey that is going to boost your money skills and turn you into a patience powerhouse.

The Savings Challenge

This is like a personal finance game where you level up by saving money. Here is how it works: Pick something cool you want to buy—maybe a new gaming console, a bike, or concert tickets. Instead of buying it right away, challenge yourself to save a bit of money each week or month toward it. Say the console costs $300, and you save $30 each week; in just 10 weeks, you will have enough to buy it! The cool part? By waiting, you learn patience and some serious savings skills, and when you finally buy it, it feels like a big win.

The 30-Day Wait Rule

This exercise will teach you to hit the pause button on impulse buys. Say you spot a killer pair of sneakers or the latest smartphone, and you are itching to buy it. Instead of jumping in, you wait 30 days. Mark it on the calendar or set a reminder. After the 30 days, if you are still as excited about it and it fits into your budget, go for it! But you might find that the urge to buy has passed or that there is something else you want more of. It is a cool way to train our brains to think about what we really value rather than just doing it for instant shopping thrills.

The Budgeting Bootcamp

This is about learning to manage your money like a boss. Each month, you set a specific amount for things like food, entertainment, and clothes. Think of it as your spending allowance. Once you hit that limit, there will be no more spending on those extras for the rest of the month. It is tough, but it teaches you to prioritize and make smart choices with your cash. For instance, do you need to eat burgers with friends tonight, or should you allocate that money toward a weekend trip to the movies? It's your call, commander!

The Impulse Spending Log

This exercise is like being a detective on your own spending habits. Every time you get the urge to buy something on a whim, jot it down in a log. Note what it was, how much it cost, and what made you want to buy it. After a while, you will start to see patterns. You may feel tempted to make purchases when you are out with friends or scrolling through social media. This log helps you understand your spending triggers so you can outsmart those impulse buys. It is like decoding your own financial mystery.

The Financial Goal-Setting Drill

This exercise can help you map out your managed missions. Start by setting a big financial goal, like saving for a car or a trip. Break this goal into smaller, more manageable targets, like saving a certain amount each month. As you hit each mini-goal, give yourself a pat on the back. This drill is about turning your big dreams into doable steps. It keeps you focused and pumped because every mini-goal you hit is a step closer to the big prize. It is goal-setting, teen-style—fun, achievable, and totally rewarding.

Definitely give these exercises a try! Think of them as mental gymnastics, preparing you for the consumerist marathons life's going to throw at you. It is not just about saving money; it is about building a mindset that helps you make smart choices in a world that is always trying to get you to spend. So, strengthen your cognitive abilities and prepare yourself to effectively navigate the financial obstacles that life presents.

THE SCRIBE OF SMART SPENDING: CHRONICLING YOUR FINANCIAL CHOICES

Picture the ancient scholars and scribes hunched over their scrolls, meticulously documenting every bit of knowledge. Now, think of yourself as a modern-day scribe, but instead of chronicling epic tales, you are tracking your spending habits. Just like those scholars, you are gathering valuable information, but it's all about where your money is going. Keeping a record of your expenses is like writing your own financial story. It is not just numbers and receipts; it is the story of your financial choices, habits, and ultimately, your journey towards being a smart spender. So, grab your pen (or phone app!) and start writing your money tale.

Becoming a Smart Spender

Becoming a "smart spender" is like transforming into a wise sage who questions every bit of information shared with them. It starts with keeping a record of every purchase. Each time you buy something, jot it down, and later, play the role of a detective, scrutinizing each expense. Ask yourself: *Did I really need this? Could I have gotten it cheaper elsewhere? Was it worth it?*

You will often find surprises, like subscriptions you forgot about but are still paying for. These unnoticed expenses are like tiny leaks in a ship—small but capable of sinking your savings over time. By identifying and eliminating them, you are not just saving money; you are stopping these leaks from draining your financial future.

So, start chronicling your spending. You will gain insights into your habits, uncover unnecessary expenses, and learn to spend wisely. It is a journey of self-discovery where you learn about your spending personality and how you can overcome challenges to become a financial success story.

Now you have the quill that determines your financial fate. Every smart spending decision you make is like penning a line in your own adventure story. Whether it is saying "no" to that extra snack or "see you later" to a subscription you never use, each choice adds up. By taking charge of your spending, you are crafting a story where you are the hero, not the sidekick, in your money saga.

In this chapter, you have seen how to become a pro at decoding the illusions and navigating the mirages of consumerism. Now imagine taking it to the next level. What if those pennies you have carefully saved could do more than just sit idle? What if they could grow, multiply, and transform into a towering fortress of financial stability? In the next chapter, *Income and Investment Alchemy*, we will dive into the magical world of investing. It is all about turning your pocket change into a powerful financial force. Get ready to learn how smart investing can turbocharge your savings into an impressive arsenal for your future.

HELP LIGHT ANOTHER TEEN'S FINANCIAL PATH

MAKE A DIFFERENCE WITH YOUR REVIEW

"No one is useless in this world who lightens the burdens of another."

— CHARLES DICKENS

People who give without expectation live longer, happier lives and make more money. So, if we've got a shot at that during our time together, darn it, I'm gonna try.

To make that happen, I have a question for you...

Would you help a fellow teen chart their course in the vast ocean of personal finance, even if you never meet them?

Think of them as a younger version of yourself – eager, hopeful, and looking for guidance.

Our mission is simple yet profound: to make financial independence a reality for every teen. But to achieve this mission, we need to reach...well..everyone. And you, dear reader, are the compass that can guide us there.

Most people do, in fact, judge a book by its cover (and reviews), so your words can make a real difference. They can be the nudge that helps another teen open this book and embark on a journey toward financial independence.

Please take a moment to share your thoughts and leave a review. It's a small gesture for you, but it could be a giant leap for another teen's financial future. Your review might inspire...

- ...a future entrepreneur to start their first business.
- ...a young driver to save up for their first car.
- ...a student to wisely stay out of debt.
- ...a dreamer to turn their vision into reality.

To leave your review, just scan this QR code:

If the thought of helping a teen you've never met brings you joy, then you're already part of our tribe. Together, we're not just reading a book; we're building a movement.

Thank you for joining us on this mission. Your support is more than just appreciated – it's a catalyst for change.

   - Your biggest supporter, Jesse

P.S. - Remember, every piece of advice you share makes you a mentor in someone else's story. If you know a teen who could benefit from this book, don't hesitate to pass it on. Let's spread the wisdom!

PILLAR 4: GENERATING WEALTH

INCOME AND INVESTMENTS

The stock market is a device for transferring money from the impatient to the patient.

— WARREN BUFFET

8

MONEY MAGIC: YOUR PLAYBOOK FOR GROWING WEALTH

Just like how tiny acorns grow into mighty oaks, your pocket change has the potential to grow into something monumental. Once you have saved up enough money to cover between three and six months of expenses, it is time to look into growing your money even faster by making wise investments.

In this chapter, we are going to explore how those spare coins and dollars can be the seeds of your financial empire. Get ready to embark on a journey where we transform your small savings into big opportunities. Let's unlock the secrets to turning your money into your ticket to financial freedom.

THE FUTURE MILLIONAIRE: TRANSFORMING POCKET CHANGE INTO GOLD

Picture medieval alchemists in their mysterious labs, surrounded by strange bottles and smoldering cauldrons, tirelessly working to turn ordinary metals into pure gold. They were pursuing a magical transformation out of curiosity and the prospect of wealth. Fast forward to today, and we have our own kind of alchemy: investing. It does not involve cauldrons or mysterious potions, but this is magic that actually works! Transform your pocket change—the money that might otherwise disappear into snacks, old subscriptions, or forgotten corners—into a valuable treasure. With the right strategies, even the smallest amount of money can grow over time, like turning lead into gold.

Think of investing as a game where patience and strategy win. By learning about stocks, bonds, and other investment options, you start to see how money can work for you, earning more money. It is not about having loads of cash to start with; it is about making smart choices with what you have. This modern alchemy is not just for the rich of the old; it is a power play available to everyone, including you. So, let's discover how to turn your pocket change into a golden future!

The Medieval Bazaar of Modern Investing

Investing is a crucial piece of your financial blueprint, almost like equipping yourself for an epic adventure. Starting early just gives you a head start. Picture the stock market as a bustling medieval bazaar. It is filled with various stalls (companies) where you can buy a piece of action (**stocks**). Over time, as the merchant does more business, your piece grows and gains in value.

Then there are **bonds**; this is like lending money to the bazaar's organizers (governments or companies) with the promise they will pay you back with interest—a safer yet less adventurous route. **Commodities** are the raw goods traded in the market, like gold, oil, or grains. **Real estate**, on the other hand, is like owning a part of the bazaar itself. It can be a more substantial investment but with the potential for rental income and value appreciation. Each of these investment types comes with its own risks and rewards, and learning about them is like learning the rules of the bazaar. Knowledge and strategy are key to navigating this exciting world.

Types of Investments

Stocks

Buying stocks means buying a small piece of a company. If the company performs well, the value of your shares might increase, and you could make a profit if you decide to sell them. For example, let's say you buy shares in a tech company because you believe it will grow. If the company launches a successful new product, the stock price might go up, increasing the value of your investment. But remember, stocks can also lose value if the company does not do well, making them a riskier investment choice.

Bonds

Bonds are a bit like giving a loan to a company or the government. When you buy a bond, you are lending money to the bond issuer for a set period of time. In return, they promise to pay you back the full amount later, plus regular interest payments along the way. For example, if you buy a bond from a city government, you are helping fund projects like building schools or roads. In return, you get regular interest payments, and when the bond matures, you get your original investment stock back. Bonds are generally considered safer than stocks, but they usually offer lower returns.

Mutual Funds

Mutual funds are like a financial team sport. When you invest in a mutual fund, you are pooling your money with other investors. A professional manager then uses this pool to buy a diverse mix of stocks, bonds, and other securities. It is a great way to get a balanced portfolio without having to buy lots of different stocks or bonds yourself. For example, if you invest in a mutual fund that focuses on tech companies, your money goes into shares from a variety of tech firms. This diversification can help reduce risk, making mutual funds a popular choice for new and young investors.

Exchange-Traded Funds (ETFs)

These are like a magical chest for our investments. They are a type of fund that holds a bunch of different investments, like stocks, bonds, or commodities, and they trade on stock exchanges, just like individual stocks. The magic part? They let you diversify your investment easily, which is like spreading your treasure across different chests, reducing the risk of putting all your gold in one place. Plus, they are usually cheaper than buying a bunch of individual stocks. Vanguard funds are a great place to begin; some popular options include:

- **VOO (Vanguard S&P 500 ETF):** Tracks the S&P 500, giving you exposure to 500 of the largest U.S. companies.
- **VTI (Vanguard Total Stock Market ETF):** Offers broad exposure to the entire U.S. stock market.
- **VEA (Vanguard FTSE Developed Markets ETF):** Focuses on stocks from developed countries outside the U.S.
- **VYM (Vanguard High Dividend Yield ETF):** Targets companies that pay higher-than-average dividends.
- **BND (Vanguard Total Bond Market ETF):** Invests in a wide spectrum of public, investment-grade U.S. bonds.

For a teen stepping into the world of investing, ETFs can be a great way to start building their treasure trove!

THE WIZARD'S WAND: THE BEGINNING INVESTOR'S TOOLKIT

Apps and banks are like a wizard's wand, an essential tool for investment magic to work. These tools give you the power to buy stocks, bonds, and mutual funds right from your phone or computer. For example, apps like Robinhood, GreenLight, or Acorns are super user-friendly, perfect for beginner wizards investing. They make buying and selling shares as easy as sending a text. Then, there are investment banks like Vanguard or Fidelity, offering a broader range of investments with a bit more magic (like advice and research). It is all about finding the right wand for investing!

Investing Apps for Teens

Greenlight App

This app is awesome for younger teens and even kids. It is not just about investing; it also teaches you about spending and saving smartly. Your parents have control over the account, but you get a debit card to make purchases, which they can monitor. Plus, they can set up chores and jobs for you to earn money! When it comes to investing, Greenlight lets you choose stocks or funds to invest in, with your parents' approval, of course. It is a great way to start learning about money in a fun, interactive way.

Fidelity Youth Account

This account is a tool for teens aged 13 to 17. It allows you to try out investing with real money, but rest assured, it is completely safe and controlled. Your parents can keep an eye on what you are doing, but you get to make the investment decisions. There are no account fees or minimums to worry about, and you get your own debit card. Plus, Fidelity offers lots of educational resources to help you learn as you go. It is like having training wheels for investing, giving you a taste of managing money before you are on your own.

Acorns Early

This is a super cool app for starting your investment journey, even when you are really young. It is part of the Acorns app, which rounds up your (or your parents') purchases to the nearest dollar and invests that spare change. With Acorns Early, your parents can set up an account for you, and Acorns invests your spare change into kid-friendly portfolios. It is a neat way to watch your money grow over time, like planting a tiny seed and watching it turn into a big, strong tree. Plus, it is a fun way to learn about investing and saving for the future.

EarlyBird

EarlyBird is a unique investing app that lets your family and friends get in on the action. Your parents can set up your investment account, and your family and friends can contribute money to it. It is like getting gifts that grow over time instead of the usual birthday or holiday presents. You can use EarlyBird for any big financial goal you might have in the future, like college or even starting your own business. It is a great way to get a head start on saving, and it is also pretty cool to see your loved ones supporting your financial future!

UNest

Unest is an app that makes saving for big future goals, like college, super easy and accessible. Your parents can set up an account for you and begin investing money in a mix of funds. The cool part? As long as you use the money for education-related expenses, it grows tax-free. It is like having a savings pot that gets bigger and bigger over time, specifically for your future education. Plus, other family members can chip in too, making it a group effort to invest in your dreams!

WeBull

WeBull is an app for the more adventurous teen investors out there. It is a step up from basic investing apps, offering a platform to trade stocks, options, and even cryptocurrencies. It is great for older teens who want to explore a wider range of investment options and dive deeper into the world of finance. WeBull provides advanced tools like analytical data and charting capabilities, which is perfect if you are serious about learning how the stock market works. Just keep in mind that it is for when you are ready to level up your investing game.

Teen Investing Made Easy

Starting to invest as a teen, even with just $100, can be both exciting and rewarding. Here are some steps to get you going:

- **Choose the right platform**: Apps like Robinhood or Acorns allow you to start investing in small amounts.
- **Set up an account**: You might need a parent or guardian to help set this up if you are under 18.
- **Learn the basics**: Understand the basics of stocks, bonds, and mutual funds.
- **Start small**: Begin with a small amount you are comfortable with, like $100.
- **Diversify**: Don't put all your money in one stock. Spread it out to reduce the risk.
- **Monitor and learn**: Keep an eye on your investments and learn as you go. Remember, it is about the long-term journey.

- **Be patient**: Investing is a marathon, not a sprint. Give your investments time to grow.

With the right "wand" or investment tool, anyone can master the intricate magic of investing. Whether you are a novice or on your way to becoming a seasoned wizard, the key is to start with the right platform and approach. Remember, investing comes with risks, but you can manage them through diversification—spreading your investments across different types of assets. This way, if one investment doesn't perform well, the others can help balance it out. With patience, the right tools, and smart strategy, you can navigate the exciting world of investing and watch your finances grow.

THE MAGIC OF COMPOUND INTEREST

Imagine you plant a small tree (this is your initial investment). As the tree grows, it not only gets taller but also sprouts new branches. Each new branch can grow its own set of leaves (these are like the interest on your original investment). Over time, the small tree becomes a giant because it is not only the trunk that has grown, but all the branches and leaves have grown with it. This is how compound interest works on your savings: Your initial amount grows, and the interest it earns grows as well, leading to a much larger sum over time, just like a fully grown, giant tree in the forest...all from a tiny seed.

Think of saving $1,000 at an interest rate of 8% per year. The first year, you earn 8% interest. Instead of taking it out, you leave it in the account. The next year, you earn interest on $1,080, and it keeps growing. By the time you are ready for college or a car, that initial $1000 could have grown significantly, all thanks to the patience and magical power of compound interest.

Let's say you save that $1,000 at the age of 16, put it into a retirement account, and let it sit until you're ready to retire – age 67. Assuming an annual return of 9%, that $1,000 has grown into a whopping $96,820! Let's do better. If you can add just $300 a month to that amount after the initial $1,000, then that grows to over $3 Million Dollars! This is the closest thing to real-life magic in the financial world. Learn to harness the power of compound interest, and your financial future will be secure. Time is your greatest asset, so save early and save often!

In conclusion, the magic of compound interest, much like any powerful enchantment, can be a potent ally or a malevolent force, depending on how you wield it. When used in investments, it multiplies your wealth, growing steadily and majestically over time like a tree turning from a seed into one of the giants in the forest. However, in the world of debts, this same magic works against you, magnifying what you owe. So, wield this magic wisely, young wizards, and let it work its magic to your benefit and not for the benefit of others.

As the curtains close on our chapter on investments and the magic of compound interest, we set the stage for an exciting new adventure. You have discovered a secret tactic, and although it seems to be magic, you can start doing it today with the tools in this chapter. Just start; the rest is easy!

But what happens when the world doesn't readily hand you the magical ingredients and resources you need for your financial endeavors? In the next chapter, we will dive into the art of foraging for these elements in the real world to generate income, even when the odds seem daunting. Get ready to learn how to navigate these challenges and turn them into opportunities for financial growth and success.

9

MAKING MONEY: THE POWER OF HUSTLE AND HEART

In the financial race of life, remember, where you start isn't where you have to finish. It is time to lace up and dive into the world of earning money. We are not just talking about main jobs but also side hustles, clever gigs, and smart hacks that can speed up your journey toward financial success. Whether you are starting from scratch or looking to boost your income, this chapter is about fueling your hustle with heart, determination, and savvy strategies. Get ready to explore new paths and sprint toward that finish line!

THE UNDERDOG'S TALE: SAVING MONEY AGAINST THE ODDS

Imagine being an underdog, someone who starts with little and faces uphill financial battles every day. I want to tell you about Leonardo Del Vecchio, a man who rose from humble beginnings. Due to his widowed mother's inability to raise him, he was sent to an orphanage, having been born into poverty. Despite these challenges, Del Vecchio dreamed big dreams and never gave up. He started as an apprentice in a factory, learned the craft of making eyewear, and eventually founded Luxottica, the world's largest producer of glasses and frames, including brands like Oakley and Ray-Ban. His story is a powerful testament to the fact that your starting point does not define your finish line. Like Del Vecchio, you, too, can rise above difficult circumstances, using grit, determination, and creativity to forge your own path to success.

Secrets to Your Success

Having a steady job, regardless of the income level, is crucial. It provides a reliable stream of income for paying bills and saving money. This could involve working part-time at a local diner, running a small business, mastering a trade such as electrical work or welding, or exploring fields like computer programming or digital marketing. Each job represents a step towards achieving financial stability. For students and aspiring professionals, internships are an excellent option. They allow you to earn while learning and gain practical experience in your field of interest. Consider this primary source of income as the anchor of your financial ship, keeping you steady as you navigate through life's challenges.

Frugal living is essential for anyone seeking financial independence. It is like a skilled mountaineer scaling a steep and rugged peak. Each penny saved and each frugal choice made is a step upward on this challenging ascent. Employing money-saving hacks, like using coupons, buying secondhand, or cooking at home, are your tools and gear, aiding in your climb. The resilience needed to save money, especially when it feels like the world is against you, is the same as the mountaineer's tenacity and grit. Every small triumph, be it skipping a needless purchase or finding a bargain, feels monumental, as if you have conquered yet another daunting cliff on your way to the summit. These achievements, no matter how small, add up to a grand victory, a testament to your determination and financial savvy.

Here are some tips to help you live frugally and spend less than you make:

- **Budget wisely**: As we have seen in the previous chapter, it is all about knowing what you spend and setting limits for your spending.
- **Avoid impulse buys**: Wait for a few days before making a purchase.
- **Cook at home**: It is cheaper (and healthier) than eating out.
- **Use student discounts**: Always ask for student discounts where they are available.
- **Secondhand shopping**: Explore thrift stores for clothes and other items.
- **Public transport and biking**: Save on gas and parking fees.
- **Sell unused items**: Declutter and make some extra cash.
- **Limit expensive hobbies**: Find low-cost or free hobbies.
- **DIY projects**: Learn to repair and create things yourself.
- **Library over buying books**: Use your local library for books and movies.

Being financially resilient means having the courage to get up and try again when things get tough. Start by setting some good goals you can get excited about. Maybe you are saving for a car, college, or a gaming console. Whatever it is, having goals gets you focused. Next up, live within your means—basically, spend less cash than you earn. It is like playing a strategy game where you have to make the most of your resources.

The first part of this arsenal should be an emergency fund. Even a little bit saved each month can be a lifesaver when unexpected stuff pops up. Any debts? Tackle them head-on, especially those pesky, high-interest ones. Try using Dave Ramsey's debt snowball method—this is a great process to kill debt (Ramsey Solutions, 2021).

The strategies we covered in this book will help you start your financial journey with the right mindset, saving habits, and investing know-how, and this is just the beginning. It is super important to keep this momentum going. As you grow and step out into the world, continue to learn and adapt. Whether it is through books (like this one), real-life experiences, or online resources like teachteensfinance.com keep expanding your financial knowledge.

Even in the toughest financial situations, remember, there is always a way to build your stash of hidden treasure—savings. With tenacity, smart strategies, and a bit of creativity, you can turn even the smallest earnings into a growing treasure chest. It is all about being clever with your money, cutting costs where you can, and sticking to your goals. Every penny you save is a victory and a step toward a more secure and stable financial future. Keep at it, and you will be amazed at what you can achieve.

THE MERCENARY'S GUIDE: NAVIGATING THE GIG ECONOMY AND SIDE JOBS

Welcome to the wild world of the gig economy and side jobs, a place that is a bit like a video game, where you can pick up quests for extra cash. It is flexible, exciting, and full of chances to rack up some serious coin. But just like any epic game, there are challenges and sneaky traps you must watch out for. In this section, we will guide you through this adventure, showing you how to snag the best gigs, dodge the not-so-great ones, and make your side hustle journey epic!

Side hustles have always been around, but they have evolved big time. Back in the day, it was all about waiting tables, crafting for fairs, fixing cars, walking dogs, or mowing lawns. Today, the game's changed with the digital world. You have options like computer programming, data entry, digital art, or even 3D print-ing. But hey, the classics are still cool—mowing lawns, selling crafts (hello, Etsy!), and dog walking are still in play. The best part? It doesn't matter what you choose. Diving into something new and earning extra cash, no matter how small, can be a total game-changer!

Imagine diving into a sprawling open-world game where every weekend freelancing gig or nighttime job is an exciting quest. The possibilities to boost your income are endless and thrilling.

- **Selling online**: Hunt for treasures at a yard sale and sell them on eBay at a profit; create your own crafts and products; or print your own photos as prints (you can even use AI) and sell them on Etsy.
- **Online tutoring**: Share your academic strengths by tutoring others online. Or if you are good at sports, why

not teach others your secrets? It is a quest to spread knowledge and learn along the way.

- **Freelance content writing**: Unleash your creativity in writing articles and blogs or reviewing other people's work. Each piece is a quest in storytelling, with payment as your reward.
- **Selling old electronics for cash**: Got an unused phone, laptop, or gaming console? You can sell it on platforms like eBay, Swappa, or Gazelle or explore Amazon's trade-in option, where you can get gift cards in exchange for your gadgets.
- **Online surveys (Branded Surveys, Scrambly, Swagbucks)**: Share your opinions on everything, from movies to snacks. Each survey is a mini-mission, rewarding you with points or cash.

These are just a few options for unique adventures in the vast world of side hustles, offering both fun and financial rewards.

And remember, side hustles are not just about making extra cash. They are a playground for honing new skills, making cool connections, and carving your own unique path in life. How you use your free time is totally up to you. Sure, binge-watching Netflix or scrolling through social media can be tempting, but imagine using the time to learn something new, create multiple income streams, and build the future you dream of. It is about seizing those moments, challenging yourself, and stepping into a world of endless possibilities. So, gear up, dive in, and start crafting the life you want—one side hustle at a time.

Create a Resume to Be Proud Of

Some of the jobs or side hustles you'll encounter require that you do an interview or require a resume. A resume is like your personal highlight reel for jobs, showing your skills, experiences, and achievements to potential employers. Creating an attractive resume is key to opening doors to new opportunities. Here are some tips:

- **Keep it simple and neat**: Choose a clean, professional layout. Use fonts like Arial or Times New Roman and organize sections clearly.
- **Highlight relevant experience**: Include part-time jobs, internships, or any work experience relevant to the job you are applying for.
- **Include extracurricular activities**: Detail your involvement in clubs, sports, or community service. It shows you are well-rounded and proactive.
- **Add a personal touch**: Write a brief personal statement at the top, summarizing your aspirations and what makes you unique.
- **Awards and honors**: Mention any academic or extracurricular awards to showcase your achievements.

Your resume is a key to unlocking exciting opportunities, so present yourself in the best possible light.

Ace a Job Interview

Now that you have a resume, it's time to ace the job interview! Getting ready for a job interview can feel like preparing for a big performance. It is your chance to show why you are the best fit for the role. Nailing the interview is about more than just showing up;

it is about presenting the best version of yourself. Think of it as a spotlight moment where you get to shine and impress. Let's dive into some ace strategies to help you rock your next job interview.

- **Dress for success**: Wear something neat and professional; it makes a great first impression.
- **Be on time**: Arrive a little early. It shows you are serious and respectful of their time. Remember, early is on time, and on time is late.
- **Body language**: Keep eye contact, smile, and have a firm handshake. It shows confidence.
- **Prepare questions**: Have a couple of questions ready about the job or company. It shows you are thoughtful and engaged.
- **Practice interviews**: Do mock interviews with friends or family to get comfortable with answering questions.
- **Post-interview, thank you**: Send a quick email or note thanking them for the opportunity. It is polite and keeps you in their mind.

Remember, confidence and preparation are key! Good luck!

LESSONS FROM A HUMBLE CHILDHOOD: WISDOM WRAPPED IN ANECDOTES

In the warmth of a North Carolina summer, my childhood was more than play; it was my first foray into the world of hard work and finance. To ensure our family's needs were met, my father juggled several jobs with relentless dedication. Inspired by his resilience, I began my own journey of earning when I was a teenager like you. My parents didn't have a lot of money, so if I wanted to go out with friends or needed gas money, I had to earn it myself.

Our family's oyster garden was my first venture. Nestled in the tranquil waters, it was more than a patch of the sea; it was a treasure trove of opportunity. My brother and I would wade through the water, harvesting oysters and clams, feeling the rough shells and the cool water, a stark contrast to the blistering sun overhead. Each oyster or clam we plucked was a lesson in patience and effort. We sold our catch to the local oyster house, and I still remember the pride I felt with every sale. It was a realization that effort could indeed turn into monetary gain. The oysters weren't just sea creatures; they were symbols of diligence turning into dollars.

My journey didn't stop at the water's edge. I joined my dad in preparing houses for painting. Scraping off old paint under the relentless sun, I learned about perseverance and the value of a hard-earned dollar. These experiences weren't just about making money; they were my early lessons in financial responsibility and saving for the future. This was the beginning of my growth mindset—that if I tried something, I could find a way to make money and support myself. After successfully earning some small dollars at these "side gig" type jobs, I found a job making pizzas at the local pizza shop. Flipping pizza dough was a dirty job; the dough got everywhere! However, this became my "main job" and allowed me to save even more money to work toward attending college. Each drop of sweat, every oyster harvested, every paint chip scraped, and every pizza flipped was a step toward my education. Saving for college was my goal, and even with three jobs, there needed to be more. Grants and student loans became part of my journey, but a solid mentality formed in my mind that I could do it!

To every teen reading this, know that your journey to financial independence may start small, but with the mindset that we cover in the first chapters of this book, the tactics and strategies we teach you here, and some perseverance, even oysters and paint chips can pave your path to success.

As we wrap up this chapter, you now know how to get started in the art of hustle and pour your heart into every effort. But what is the end game? In the upcoming chapter, we will look into the future, imagining a world shimmering with the rewards of your hard work. It is all about balancing the daily grind with your long-term dreams; make sure you stay on course and that every step you take today paves the way for a brighter, more secure tomorrow. Let's get ready to look forward and map out the path to our golden future!

10

THE GOLDEN FUTURE

I magine if you could hop into a time machine and shake hands with your future self, who is living it up as a millionaire. Sounds cool, right? Today, we are going to use the magic of compound interest and master the art of long-term planning. This chapter is all about understanding why starting early can make a massive difference and how you can set the stage now for a future filled with financial freedom and success.

Let me share Eric Zhao's story with you; it is a powerful tale of foresight and determination. At 15, living in Albuquerque, New Mexico, Eric is already very aware of the importance of financial security, a lesson he learned through his family's experiences. His parents, immigrants from China, faced numerous financial challenges, including a six-figure hospital bill for Eric after a severe accident at age nine. This experience, along with seeing his sister graduate with $30,000 in student loans, has driven Eric to save diligently. Working at his parents' acupuncture clinics, he saves 50% of his earnings, aiming to accumulate $10,000 to diversify his investments in retirement accounts, stocks, and bonds (Mitra, 2020). The best news is that you can do this too!

In the next sections, we are going to explore the mysteries of retirement funds and how you can make them work for you now!

MAGICAL TREASURE CHESTS: UNLOCKING THE MYSTERIES OF 401(K)S AND IRAS

These acronyms (401k, IRA, Roth), cryptic as ancient runes, are keys to unlocking a prosperous retirement. Imagine these accounts as magical chests where your contributions grow, shielded by the powers of tax advantages and compound interest. Join me as we unravel these mysteries, decoding how each plan works and how they can be your allies in creating a future filled with financial security and abundance.

Let's journey together through the labyrinth of retirement funds, transforming complex jargon into easy, relatable terms. From the familiar 401(k) to IRAs of various kinds, each path holds unique advantages and considerations. As we navigate this maze, you will gain clarity and insight, equipping you with the knowledge to make wise decisions for your financial future. Are you ready to decode these mysteries?

Roth IRA

A Roth IRA is like a savings account for your future self, with a twist:

- **How it works**: You contribute after-tax money. The magic happens as your money grows tax-free, and you can withdraw it tax-free in retirement.

- **Pros**: Since you have already paid taxes on your contributions, everything you withdraw later (including the earnings) is yours to keep; there are no extra taxes.
- **Cons**: There is no immediate tax break on your contributions, unlike a traditional IRA.
- **Contribution limits**: Similar to the traditional IRA, it is $7,000 per year.

For teens, a Roth IRA is a cool way to start saving early, giving you plenty of time to grow. Plus, tax-free withdrawals in retirement are a big win!

The 401(k) Plan

Employers mostly offer this plan, which acts as a piggy bank for your older self. Here is how it rolls:

- **How it works**: You contribute a portion of your paycheck before taxes are taken out. This money then gets invested in stocks, bonds, or mutual funds.
- **Pros**: Your contributions lower your taxable income now, and you get tax-deferred growth, meaning you don't pay taxes until you withdraw the money in retirement.
- **Cons**: There are penalties for early withdrawal, and investment options are limited to what the plan offers.
- **Contribution limits**: Currently, the limit is $23,00 per year for those under 50.

If you are working a job that offers a 401(k), joining early can kickstart your savings. Even small contributions can grow significantly over time, thanks to compound interest. Most companies will offer a matching contribution, so they will put the same amount of money you put in – this is free money! It's best to put in at least up to the employer match to maximize your savings!

Simple IRA and Simple 401(k)

Simple IRA and Simple 401(k) are like starter kits for small business retirement plans. These plans are great for teens working in small businesses, offering a simple way to start saving for retirement early on:

- **How they work**: Designed for small businesses, they allow both employers and employees to contribute.
- **Pros**: They are easier and less costly to administer than traditional 401(k)s, with straightforward rules.
- **Cons**: Contribution limits are lower than other retirement accounts, and early withdrawal penalties can be steep.
- **Contribution limits**: For a simple IRA, it is up to $16,000; for a simple 401(k), the limit is $23,000.

The contribution limits above are current as of the time of publication. These limits may be increased over time to allow you to save more. Keep an eye out for those limit increases so you can take advantage of them!

Now, it is time for you to choose your own path and begin to shape your own financial future in retirement. Whether it is the steady growth of a 401(k), the tax-free benefits of a Roth IRA, or the flexibility of a solo 401(k) for the entrepreneurial spirit, the choice is yours. Talk with your parents and your bank, and as a teen, you'll likely want to get started with a Roth IRA and one or two ETFs (as we discussed earlier in the book)!

CRAFTING YOUR FUTURE: HOW TO START PLANNING NOW

Imagine walking through a magical portal and meeting your future self, financially secure and thriving. This is not just fantasy; it is a future you can create! The practices of saving and investing are like the tools in a craftsman's kit for building your financial future. Each tool in your financial toolkit—be it savings accounts, investment strategies, or budget plans—serves as an instrument in laying the foundation and erecting the walls of your future financial stronghold. Every dollar saved and intelligently invested today is like a carefully placed brick in the foundation of your future success. Begin building now, using these tools with precision and foresight. Watch as your future self emerges just as you saw them, sculpted from your wise choices and unwavering dedication to your financial goals.

Planning for your golden future might seem daunting, but starting early is key. Think of it as an adventure:

- **Time is your biggest advantage:** Starting to save and invest as a teen can lead to a huge payoff due to compound interest. It is like planting a tree early so you can enjoy its shade sooner.
- **Make saving a habit:** Like any good habit, saving money regularly, even in small amounts, builds a strong financial foundation.
- **Financial literacy is power:** Understand money management basics. It is a tool richer than gold for making smart financial decisions.
- **Focus on building assets:** Invest in things that grow in value over time, like property (assets) over luxury items (liabilities).

- **Education and career choices matter:** Choose a career path that is in demand and manage education loans wisely.
- **Automate and innovate:** Think about creating systems or businesses that can generate income without your constant presence (passive income).

As we close this chapter, having glimpsed your golden future and harnessed the skills of retirement funds and compound interest, a new challenge awaits. Are you ready to wield the double-edged sword of credit, to dance on the knife edge of risk and reward? In our next chapter, we will venture into the perilous waters of debt. Here, you will learn the art of balancing credit wisely and understanding its potential and pitfalls. Prepare your wits and courage as we navigate through the stormy seas of debt management and financial responsibility.

PILLAR 5

HIDDEN DANGERS

Debt is like any other trap, easy enough to get into, but hard enough to get out of.

— HENRY WHEELER SHAW

11

CREDIT AND DEBT: NAVIGATING THE DOUBLE-EDGED SWORD

In this chapter, we will explore the dual nature of credit and debt—the Dr. Jekyll and Mr. Hyde of finance. Understanding how to build and maintain good credit is crucial; it opens doors to opportunities but can also lead to pitfalls if not managed wisely. Navigating the world of debt requires skill and knowledge. Let's explore the intricacies of partnering effectively with credit and debt, avoiding any potential pitfalls. By mastering this, you will be on your way to maintaining a healthy financial life.

THE SIREN'S SONG: THE ALLURE AND DANGER OF CREDIT

Picture credit as a powerful but deceptive temptress, a siren in the sea of finance. Her song is captivating, promising dazzling opportunities and conveniences. Like the siren's call, a good credit score can lead you to the shores of fortune, unlocking doors on loans, mortgages, and lower interest rates. But, just like sailors lured by the siren's song, it is a dance that can lead to the perils of debt if not navigated with care. This allure of debt, while enticing, demands respect and understanding, for it holds the power to shape your financial journey towards prosperity or doom.

Credit history is like a melody, where each financial decision you make is a note that echoes through your life. Every credit card purchase, loan taken, or bill paid on time contributes to the total. If you manage your credit wisely, hitting the right notes by paying bills on time and using credit responsibly, you create a harmonious tune that boosts your credit score. But miss a few notes, like late payments or high credit card balances, and the melody can become discordant, affecting your ability to get loans or favorable interest rates in the future. Just like a melody, your credit history tells a story; make it a beautiful one.

Credit scores are like the vibrant colors in a financial painting, crucial in shaping the big picture of your life. Imagine wanting to buy your dream home or kickstart a business. Your credit score acts like a beacon, signaling to lenders how trustworthy you are with money. A high score, glowing with financial reliability, can open doors to better mortgages or loans with lower interest rates, making these life-changing events more accessible and affordable. On the flip side, a lower score can dim these prospects, making it harder and more expensive to borrow money if you ever need it.

It is important to understand the consequences of bad credit. Think of it as a dark undertow in the ocean of finance. Just as a hidden current can pull an unwary swimmer under, bad credit can drag you into a vortex of financial woes. It can lead to high-interest rates on loans, difficulty securing housing, and even affect job opportunities. Managing your finances with caution is key to avoiding this perilous current and keeping your financial journey smooth and steady.

Tips to Build and Maintain a Good Credit Score

- **Start early**: The best way to build credit early is to be an authorized user on your parent's credit card. You don't even have to use it – have your parent keep it in a safe place and use your debit card for purchases. This builds your credit but removes the temptation and opportunity to overspend.
- **Use credit wisely**: Only use a small portion of your available credit.
- **Pay bills on time**: Always pay credit card bills, car payments, and other debts on time.
- **Monitor your credit score:** Check your credit report regularly for errors.
- **Limit new credit requests**: Too many credit inquiries can hurt your score.
- **Learn about credit**: Educate yourself on how credit works and financial responsibility.

Remember, building good credit is a journey, not a sprint. Start small, stay consistent, and your score will grow over time.

Best Practices for Credit Cards

Think of credit cards like a siren's call—alluring but dangerous if not handled well. It is best to avoid credit cards completely, but if you have one, then you must pay it off every month to navigate those waters with care. Here is how to do it safely:

- **Smart Spending**: Treat your credit card like cash. If you can't afford it, don't swipe it.
- **Full payoff**: Pay your balance in full each month, period! This keeps you out of debt's whirlpool and forms a foundation for responsible credit card usage. If you can't

pay for it in full at the end of the month, reconsider purchasing the item at all.

- **Low balance**: Keep your spending low; only using a bit of your credit limit helps improve your credit score. Google "credit card utilization ratio" and learn why. Ideally, a utilization ratio of 10% or less is best to target as you work to build your credit.
- **Never late**: Set alarms so you never miss a payment, avoiding late fees.
- **Know your map**: Understand your card's terms: rates, fees, and rewards.
- **Rewards**: If your card has rewards, use them, but don't let them tempt you into overspending.
- **No Annual Fee**: Only select a credit card with a $0 annual fee.

Again, it is best to avoid credit cards completely. Sail smart with your credit card, and you will steer clear of trouble!

NAVIGATING THE LABYRINTH: DEBT, LOANS, AND THE MINOTAUR WITHIN

From the winding paths of credit card debt to the deep corridors of student loans, each twist and turn of the maze represents the different types and dangers of debt. Just like a maze, debt can seem confusing, with every decision leading to potential pitfalls or safe passages. The best advice for navigating this maze is to *never enter it*; debt is not something that you should use, especially early in your financial journey. However, if it is unavoidable, you need to understand each sector of this financial labyrinth to evade the Minotaur and emerge victorious, armed with knowledge and smart strategies to conquer the complexities of debt.

Let's navigate this debt labyrinth with a light-hearted torch. Think of "good debt" as a pathway leading to treasures. There are things like student loans or mortgages where you are investing in your future. They are like secret passages that lead to new realms of knowledge.

Then there is "bad debt." These are like traps in the maze; think of high-interest credit card debt or loans for things that don't increase in value, like furniture and computers. These are the twists and turns that can lead you to the Minotaur if you are not careful.

Remember, every type of debt is a different path in the maze. Choose wisely to find the treasure and avoid the Minotaur!

Escape the Debt Labyrinth: Your Sword and Shield for Financial Freedom

Armed with the mythical sword and shield of debt management, you can escape the labyrinth. The sword is your plan to attack debt: list all your debts, prioritize them (highest interest rates first), and start paying them off methodically. Your shield represents a strategy: creating an "artificial environment of economic scarcity." It means living below your means, like you have less money than you do. This strategy helps you save more and pay off debts faster. Think of it as your guiding thread, leading you out of the maze, away from the Minotaur of debt, and into the light of financial freedom.

Conquering the Maze: The Debt Avalanche and Snowball Strategies

In your quest to conquer the debt labyrinth, two mighty strategies stand out: the "debt avalanche" and "debt snowball" methods. Picture the **debt avalanche** as an unstoppable force, targeting debts with the highest interest rate first, reducing the amount you pay over time. It is like strategically defeating the biggest monsters first.

The **snowball method** involves starting with the smallest debts and gaining momentum and confidence as each one is vanquished. It is like clearing the smaller, easier paths in the maze first, building up to the bigger challenges.

Both methods are powerful tools in your journey through the labyrinth of debt, helping you emerge victorious and debt-free!

Debt, when mismanaged, can quickly become overwhelming, trapping you in its labyrinth. So, stay vigilant, use your strategies wisely, and keep your financial goals in sight. By doing so, you will navigate through the maze of debt safely, avoiding the perilous horns of financial distress. Stay sharp, stay smart, and you will emerge victorious in the battle against debt.

STUDENT LOANS: ARE THEY WORTH IT?

Student loans can appear like a key to unlocking a future of education and opportunity, akin to a compass leading you to buried treasure. They promise enhanced career prospects and a path to a better life driven by the power of knowledge. However, this promise comes with a caveat. Just as a skilled navigator must plot a course through a rough sea, you must calculate a realistic salary post-graduation and plan your loan repayment so you're not saddled with debt for many years. Not planning wisely can lead to financial burdens rather than benefits. Let's delve into understanding student loans, ensuring they are a stepping stone to success, not a stumbling block to financial difficulty.

Student Loans: The Alchemy of Education

Student loans can be complicated and resemble ancient scrolls filled with cryptic text waiting to be deciphered. Each scroll can be a boon or a curse, unlocking education's doors or binding you to financial chains. Let's decipher these different types together and equip you to make the best decision.

Federal vs. Private Loans

The government provides federal student loans. They come with fixed interest rates, meaning the rate stays the same throughout the life of the loan. They also offer benefits like income-driven repayment plans (which set your loan payments based on your monthly income) and potential loan forgiveness programs.

Banks, credit unions, or other private entities offer private student loans. Private student loans may have fixed or variable interest rates that can change over time. They usually require a credit check and don't offer as many flexible repayment options as federal loans.

Choosing between the two is like selecting the right tool for your educational quest; each has its own set of advantages and risks.

Deciphering Interest Rates

Interest rates on student loans determine how much extra you will pay on top of the borrowed amount each time you make a payment. A lower interest rate means less extra cost over time, while a higher rate can significantly increase the total amount you repay. Federal loans typically have fixed interest rates, providing predictability. In contrast, private loans can have variable rates, which might start lower but can fluctuate, making future payments uncertain. Understanding these rates is crucial, as they affect how much you will ultimately need to pay back after your educational journey.

Pausing the Clock: Understanding Payment Deferral in Student Loans

Delving into the option of delaying payments, like finding a hidden passage in a labyrinth, reveals ways to temporarily pause your loan repayments. This comes in two forms: deferment and forbearance. Deferment is like a magical stasis, where you can postpone payments due to specific circumstances like going back to school, and often, interest does not accrue on subsidized loans during this period. Forbearance, on the other hand, is a temporary respite from payments when you face financial hardship, but interest typically continues to accumulate. Both options offer breathing room, yet they require careful consideration due to their impact on the loan's overall growth.

Mapping the Boundaries: Navigating Loan Limits in Student Financing

In the world of student loans, understanding loan limits is like knowing the boundaries of a mystical territory. Federal student loans come with set limits, defining how much you can borrow each year and in total. These limits vary based on factors like your year in school and dependency status (things like whether you live at home, are dependent on your parents, or are off on your own). Private loans, however, might offer higher amounts, but borrowing more than you need can lead to a perilous path of excessive debt. It is crucial to borrow *only what is necessary*, ensuring you don't overstep into a financial abyss from which it is hard to return.

Navigate wisely, young scholars, to harness the power of student loans without falling into despair.

Mastering the Art of Student Loan Management: Your Guide to Financial Wisdom

When it comes to managing student loans responsibly, consider harnessing the profound knowledge of financial wisdom:

- **Borrow only what you need**: This means resisting the temptation of taking out more money than is necessary for your education. Imagine packing for an adventurous journey and taking only what is essential to avoid being weighed down. Calculate your tuition, books, and living expenses, and borrow just enough to cover these costs. Remember when we talked about budgeting? This is where knowing how to budget keeps your debt load as low as possible, ensuring that you are not overburdened financially when it is time to repay.
- **Understand your loans**: Know the type of loans you have (federal or private), their interest rates, and repayment terms. Familiarize yourself with how interest accrues and what your monthly payments might look like after graduation. This knowledge empowers you to make informed decisions and plan effectively for your financial future. It is about being proactive and fully aware of the commitments you are making.
- **Plan for repayment**: Start by understanding when your repayment begins and what your monthly obligations will be. Then create a budget that includes these loan payments as a key component. Think about ways you can earn more money or cut back on your spending to comfortably meet your loan obligations. This forward-thinking approach helps you avoid financial surprises and ensures you are ready to meet your repayment responsibilities head-on. It

is about being prepared and strategic with our finances from the get-go.

- **Explore forgiveness programs**: These can be like hidden treasures that could lighten your financial load. Particularly for federal loans, there are programs like Public Service Loan Forgiveness (PSLF), which might forgive your remaining debt after you make a certain number of payments while working in the public service or non-profit sectors. It is important to research and understand the specific requirements and application processes for these programs. Seeking out these opportunities can potentially offer significant relief from student loan debt.

- **Consider refinancing**: This is like searching for a more efficient path on your financial journey. This means replacing your existing loans with a new one, ideally at a lower interest rate. It can simplify your payments by consolidating multiple loans into one and potentially lower your monthly payment or reduce the total amount paid over time. However, it is important to weigh this option carefully, especially if you have federal loans, as refinancing with a private lender may mean losing certain federal loan benefits. It is a strategic move that requires careful consideration of your current and future financial situation.

Remember, the best debt strategy is to avoid it, but if it is necessary, you now have mastered how to use it like a champion. But are you prepared for the next adventure into the mystical realm of digital alchemy? Up next, we embark on a journey into the enigmatic and ever-evolving world of cryptocurrency. Will it reveal itself as your digital goldmine, or will it prove to be the fool's gold you are chasing? Stay tuned as your journey into the heart of modern finance continues.

1 2

CRYPTO: DIGITAL TREASURE OR FOOL'S GOLD

In this chapter, we will navigate the basics of digital currencies, equipping you with the knowledge to start your journey safely. In the ever-fluctuating landscape of cryptocurrencies, understanding what you are stepping into is crucial. Do you dare tread the volatile ground of Bitcoin, Ethereum, and their kin? Together, we will sift through the complexities, separating the dazzling allure of digital treasure from the deceptive glitter of fool's gold. Let's embark on this modern financial adventure together!

THE ENCHANTED FOREST OF CRYPTOCURRENCY: MYTH OR REALITY?

Think of cryptocurrency as an enchanted forest, a mystical realm where digital gold gleams in the dappled shadows. In this forest, mythical beasts like "Bitcoin" and "Ethereum" roam, each holding the promise of untold riches. But like any enchanted forest, there is a catch: does this wonderland brim with opportunity—a place where digital fortunes are made? Or is it a dark abyss fraught with peril and uncertainty? As we venture deeper, we will explore this digital domain, seeking to uncover whether it is a land of potential treasure or a treacherous pitfall.

Enchanted Coins of the Digital Realm: Exploring Bitcoin, Ethereum, and More

In the mystical forest of cryptocurrency, imagine each digital coin as a unique artifact crafted from the magic of blockchain technology. Blockchain is like an ancient, unbreakable ledger—a series of interconnected blocks that record every transaction securely and transparently.

Cryptocurrency operates without central banks or traditional monetary systems. It is like a realm with its own rules, where transactions occur directly between individuals, overseen by the watchful eyes of the blockchain. A network of computers maintains this decentralized world, revolutionizing money, and digital transactions instead of being controlled by any single entity like the U.S. government, which controls dollars.

Let's look at some of the best-known cryptocurrencies.

Bitcoin

This is the original and most famous cryptocurrency, and it is like the grand old tree in the heart of the enchanted forest. It was a pioneer in the field of digital currencies when Satoshi Nakamoto created it in 2009. Bitcoin operates on a decentralized network using blockchain technology, making it secure and resistant to fraud. It operates under a decentralized authority, in contrast to government-issued currencies, and as a digital currency, it potentially has lower transaction fees than conventional online payment methods. Bitcoin's value has seen dramatic highs and lows, making it both a potentially lucrative investment and a risky venture.

Ethereum

Ethereum is like a multifaceted gem in the cryptocurrency forest; it goes beyond being just digital money. Launched in 2015, it is not only a platform for Ethereum's currency, Ether, but also for executing "smart contracts." These agreements are automated and do not require intermediaries, functioning like magic contracts that self-execute when conditions are met. Ethereum's blockchain also supports "Decentralized Applications (DApps)," making it a versatile ecosystem. Its ability to support complex operations has positioned it as more than just a currency, like a wizard capable of various magical feats in the digital realm.

Tether and USD Coin

Tether and USD Coin, like stable anchors in the turbulent seas of cryptocurrency, are known as "stable coins." Their value is pegged to a stable asset like the US dollar, making them unique. **Tether (USDT)** and **USD Coin (USDC)** offer the digital efficiency of cryptocurrencies while aiming to minimize price volatility. They act like a bridge between the world of traditional fiat currencies and the new digital realm, offering a steadier option for those cautious of the typical ups and downs associated with other digital currencies.

Cryptocurrency, like a mythical treasure, has aspects of both digital gold and fool's gold. It is cool because it is new and can grow in value fast, but it is also unpredictable and can change a lot. Some experts think it is a great opportunity, but they also say you should be careful because it is still pretty new and can be a kind of gamble. So, if you are thinking about jumping into the crypto world, just make sure you do your homework and don't put all your coins in one basket!

GETTING STARTED WITH CRYPTOCURRENCY SAFELY

Step into the alchemist's lab, a mystical blend of magic and science, where flasks bubble and ancient scrolls line the walls. In this enchanting place, you are about to brew your very own potion for cryptocurrency investment. Here, among the shimmering vials and cryptic tomes, lies the secret to initiating into the world of digital currencies safely. With each ingredient, blend caution with curiosity. Ready to mix and master the elixir of safe cryptocurrency investment?

Embarking on your cryptocurrency journey is like following a precise alchemy recipe. Here are the steps:

- **Do your research**: Start by understanding each crypto asset. It is like selecting the right ingredients for your potion.
- **Choose a reliable exchange**: Find a reputable platform. Think of it as your cauldron, where the magic happens. Coinbase.com is a great place to start.
- **Secure your investment**: Use strong passwords and two-factor authentication; a passkey is best. This is like sealing your potion to keep it safe.
- **Invest wisely**: Don't invest in crypto until you have your emergency savings account, six months of savings, and your retirement accounts in good working order. After those are funded, you can splurge here on crypto.
- **Stay informed**: Keep up with crypto news. It is like constantly monitoring your potion's progress.
- **Be cautious**: Remember, the crypto world is volatile. Invest only what you can afford to lose, as every alchemist knows the risk of an experiment.

As you stand ready with your newly brewed vial of crypto knowledge, sip cautiously, prepared for the spells and surprises of the digital currency world. Now, armed with essential wisdom, you can navigate your crypto journey. Remember, the world of cryptocurrency is filled with both wonder and cautionary tales. Approach each step with awareness and readiness for whatever magical twists or unforeseen curses may lie ahead.

You have traveled through enchanted forests and navigated pirate-infested waters in search of digital treasure. However, beyond the allure of riches lies a deeper quest—to enrich the soul by generously sharing treasures instead of hoarding them. Now, let's unfurl the sails of our next grand adventure: The art of giving. In this chapter, we will explore the luminous power of altruism and ethical wealth, discovering how the act of giving not only enriches others but illuminates our own lives as well. Get ready to embark on this noble journey, where true wealth is measured not in coins but in kindness.

PILLAR 6: LEVEL UP

MASTERING GENEROSITY AND YOUR FINANCIAL TOOLKIT

No one has ever become poor by giving.

— ANNE FRANK

13

THE ART OF GIVING—CREATING CIRCLES OF COMPASSION

This chapter invites you on a journey to explore the importance of ethical wealth and the power of giving. Here, we will delve into why sharing our riches creates ripples of positive change, weaving circles of compassion in our communities and beyond. By the end of this chapter, you will understand why generosity is important and have practical tools and strategies to make meaningful contributions to your community. Prepare to discover how you can help make this world a better place for us all!

TRANSFORMING WEALTH INTO HUMAN CONNECTION

Have you ever heard of the Philosopher's Stone? It is this cool mythical rock that could supposedly turn base metals like lead into gold. Now, imagine if giving was like your very own philosopher's stone, but it's not about turning metals into gold but way cooler—transforming your material wealth into human connections and ethical growth. When you give, you are not just giving away some of your money or stuff; you are giving a little bit of your time and yourself to create bonds, understanding, and a positive impact. This is real human connection, and in a world that has endured a global pandemic, being together and connecting is priceless.

Sharing wealth is not just about being nice; it is a deep philosophy behind it. Stoicism, an ancient Greek philosophy, teaches us that the real key to happiness is not getting more stuff but being content and doing good for others. It is all about understanding what we can control (like our actions and attitudes) and what we can't (like, well, pretty much everything else).

And guess what? When you share your wealth or help someone out, you are not just doing them a favor; you are also helping yourself and fueling your personal growth as a compassionate human. It feels good, right? Plus, it helps you connect with others and grow as a person. It is like leveling up in real life.

In the end, you have the incredible power to transform how you see wealth and well-being. When you give from the heart, you're not just sharing your wealth; you're cultivating generosity within, creating positive change in yourself and those around you. This cultivation—turning kindness and compassion into transformative actions—becomes the most fulfilling journey you can undertake.

THE COMPASS OF COMPASSION: HELPING OTHERS

Life is often like an unpredictable ocean adventure. Imagine your good deeds and kindness as a compass, like the one sailors use. This moral compass is your guide through all the crazy ups and downs. It reminds you to help others and spread kindness, no matter how wild the waves get. So, as you are cruising through life, remember to let your heart be your compass, pointing you towards doing good deeds for others and making a real difference.

Here are some ideas to get you thinking about how you can give back to your community:

- **Volunteer**: Find local organizations or charities that interest you and offer your time.
- **Donate**: If you can, donate money, clothes, or other items to those in need.
- **Support fundraisers**: Participate in or organize fundraisers for good causes.
- **Be a friend**: Sometimes, simple acts of kindness, like helping a neighbor, make a big difference.
- **Use your skills**: Offer your talents, like tutoring or tech skills, for free to those who could benefit from them.

Remember, every small action counts!

THE FAMILY TAPESTRY: WEAVING THREADS OF GENEROSITY

Picture a grand tapestry rich with the history of your family's generation. Each thread represents acts of kindness and ethical decisions made over time. Just as every stitch contributes to the beauty of the tapestry, every good deed you do weaves into this family legacy. It's about continuing the tradition of generosity and adding your own vibrant threads to the tapestry that tells the story of who you are and where you come from.

As you envision the tapestry you will weave for your own family, let me reveal the vibrant patterns of giving that have threaded through my family's past, offering you inspiration for your own acts of generosity.

My first memory of a family member who embodied generosity was Grandaddy Brown. He passed away when I was just 16 years old. He was the first to teach me about generosity, as he silently gave away food in our community. With his three-fingered hand, a reminder of life's impermanence and the dangers of farm plows, he would distribute the bounty of his garden to his neighbors. The loss of his fingers hindered his ability to work certain jobs, so he didn't have much money, but that didn't stop him from being generous with what he did have. Bags containing tomatoes, corn, potatoes, and peanuts would appear on doorsteps, a silent testament to his selfless nature. Walking alongside him, I learned the silent language of giving and that the reward is not recognition for doing so, but the way it makes you feel inside.

My mother, even while shadows of cancer loomed over her, knitted warmth and comfort into prayer shawls. Her hands, weaving yarn as she battled illness, were never too weary to offer solace to others. A particular shawl, crafted with love for a young girl in our church, was more than wool; it was a warm embrace as the little girl was lying scared in her hospital bed. Her generosity was a lesson that even in our darkest hours, we can shine a light for others.

My own children learned the lesson of selflessness through a Christmas unlike any other. Instead of gifts under the tree, we turned to a catalog from World Vision. My children, with gleeful hearts, chose to give the gift of goats and chickens to a village far away, learning that joy doesn't always come wrapped in a bow. Through meals for the needy, Operation Christmas Child boxes, and wells for African villages, my children learned that money's greatest value comes not from what it buys for us but from the help it provides to others. I love to teach them what Nana taught me about money: you spend some, you save some, and you must give some away.

As you think about the threads you will add to your family's tapestry, remember to weave with more than just gold—use the enduring fibers of love, integrity, and generosity.

Consider the gifts your family has and how they can be used to cultivate a spirit of generosity. You can serve food at a local shelter, feed needy families through a local church, work on community projects together, or donate to missions all over the world. Whether you knit prayer shawls like my mom or help feed those who are in need, these acts of kindness weave a tapestry of generosity into your family's life.

With the Philosopher's Stone in hand and our compass set on compassion, we have unearthed a treasure far greater than what fills bank accounts. Now, it is time to prepare for the final chapter of our adventure. Gather your quills and ready your ink; we are about to assemble your *Financial Toolkit.* This is the ultimate arsenal for your lifelong expedition into the realms of fiscal wisdom and ethical wealth. The knowledge and tools you will acquire are not just for today but for a future filled with financial savvy and moral richness.

14

BUILDING YOUR FINANCIAL
TOOLKIT

Growing up in a family with limited extra spending money, I learned the value of hard work early on. Yet, my understanding of personal finance was initially just about saving. It wasn't until college, when I encountered my first credit card and the shock of a $1,000 bill that I began to truly understand the complexities of financial management and started building my financial toolkit. This experience was my wake-up call. I delved into books at the library to understand interest rates, how credit card debt accumulates, and the importance of managing it. This knowledge was my first significant tool in financial literacy, but it also opened my eyes to the other side of interest: earning interest through investments. I didn't just have to pay interest; I could earn it!

This led me to open my first brokerage account at E*Trade, and I had another tool in my belt. Life continued to teach me valuable lessons. A friend's car accident highlighted the importance of adequate insurance, leading me to learn about different types and how to protect myself financially. As I started my career, I navigated the world of 401(k)s and Roth IRAs, realizing I had lost a decade's worth of potential earnings from compound interest toward my retirement. All of these realizations hit home when my children became teenagers and became the driving force behind this book.

I share my journey, filled with challenges and obstacles, to provide you with a head start on building a strong financial foundation. This book is not just a guide but a shortcut to financial wisdom, and it is only the beginning.

To help you build your own financial toolkit and avoid the perilous pits of despair, the list below is a treasure map of all the tools you'll need to be successful:

1. **Develop your financial mindset**: Listen to podcasts, read books, and practice the art of delayed gratification. Do hard things, and before long, those hard things will become easier. Stay off social media as much as possible; don't compare yourself to others—that's the mirage of consumerism. It's a trap!
2. **Hustle and Heart**: You need to get a job and/or a side gig. This will bring income, which is the first step in getting your foundation built. Just get started; the rest will come.
3. **Create your *safe* havens**: Open a checking and savings account so you can manage your money effectively.
4. **Master budgeting**: Get through boot camp by making a budget that balances spending, saving, and giving. Remember to allocate resources wisely by deciding whether something is a need or a want!
5. Save up to $1,000 in **emergency savings** and 3 months of expenses. This will be your safety net and give you peace when things get tough.

6. **Start investing**: Open an investing account with your bank (a "brokerage" account) and set up a Roth IRA to start. Start by trying to get $6,000 into your Roth IRA. To help with decision-making, just start by putting it into the VOO fund (see Chapter 8).

7. **Avoid the danger of debt**: Your early years should be spent saving and investing so you can earn interest. Don't pay others interest by taking out debt unless absolutely necessary.

8. **Imagine your golden future**: Use online retirement calculators to visualize your financial future and see the magic of compound interest at work. This will keep you motivated to keep saving and investing as you see that future number grow. To do all this you'll need tools, weapons, armor, and support to help you on your way. As a bonus to this book, just visit www.teachteensfinance.com to get free resources like budgeting sheets, application links and reviews, helpful tips and tricks, financial simulators, games, and more.

This book and accompanying website are all about helping you get the help you need to achieve financial freedom and independence! As we turn to the final pages of this chapter, congratulations are in order! You have journeyed through the essentials of financial literacy, from the foundations of budgeting to the intricacies of investing. Though we are nearing the end of this book, remind yourself that you are just at the starting line of your journey to financial freedom. Every page you have turned here has equipped you with the knowledge and tools to navigate your path with confidence and savvy. Keep this momentum going; your adventure toward a bright and prosperous future is only just beginning.

CONCLUSION

In this journey through the realms of financial literacy, we've navigated a sea of essential concepts, from the importance of savings and the intricacies of budgeting to the complexities of investing and the subtleties of credit. At its core, this book is about empowering you, the reader, with the tools and knowledge to build a solid financial foundation. It showed you the importance of a mindful approach to money, the value of informed decision-making, and the impact of consistent saving and investing habits.

Remember, financial literacy is not just about accumulating wealth; it is about mastering your mindset, making informed choices, living within your means, and planning for the future one step at a time. But knowledge alone isn't enough; action is the key.

The book ends here, but your journey continues. As you turn these last pages, I challenge you to take action now. I know the book has a lot in it, but you only need to take one step. Start small by setting up a savings account, creating a budget, or researching a side hustle you can pursue. As you gain confidence, venture into the world of investing and keep learning about the ever-evolving landscape of personal finance. When you get each item done, check it off the list in chapter 14.

You are not alone!

To support your ongoing quest, visit teachteensfinance.com for a wealth of free resources, tools, and further learning materials. This website is a continuation of our book, offering practical support as you apply these lessons to real-life step-by-step.

PASSING THE TORCH OF FINANCIAL WISDOM

You've journeyed through the pages of financial enlightenment and are now equipped with the tools for financial independence. It's your turn to pass on the beacon of knowledge to guide others on their path.

By sharing your honest thoughts about this book on Amazon, you become a lighthouse guiding other teens and young adults to the shores of financial wisdom. Your review is more than just words; it's a roadmap for those seeking the same insight and empowerment you've gained.

We're on a mission to spread financial literacy and independence, and your contribution is invaluable in this journey. By sharing your experience, you're not just reviewing a book; you're igniting a chain of inspiration and knowledge.

Thank you for being a vital part of this mission. Together, we're not only enriching lives; we're creating a community of financially savvy individuals. Your support in sharing your review keeps the spirit of learning and growing alive.

Every review counts, and every shared experience is a step towards a brighter, more financially empowered future for all. Let's keep the flame of financial literacy burning bright for generations to come.

Scan the QR code below

ABOUT THE AUTHOR

Born in Texas and raised on the sunny beaches of North Carolina, J.L. Davis has a strong work ethic and a resilient nature. His financial journey started when he was just twelve years old. He helped his father paint houses and harvest oysters from the family garden to earn money to spend.

Today, J.L. is the proud father of three sons and actively guides them down their own paths of financial success. This book is one way he's capturing that journey to share with teens everywhere. He started his corporate career as a software engineer and ended up as a Chief Operating Officer, leading the overall operations and financial management of several leading tech companies. Despite these accomplishments, he encountered many challenges. He made several mistakes on his personal financial journey and knows firsthand the dangers and rewards of mismanaging finances. He's been in the trenches of student loans and credit card debt. Fortunately, he had mentors who could guide him in navigating the complexities of personal finance during his college years, allowing him to learn good money management skills while young so he could get back on track.

Today, J.L. is eager to share what he learned with the next generation to help them accelerate their own path to financial independence. He believes that financial freedom is not an impossible dream. Armed with the proper knowledge, mindset, and practices, it is within everyone's reach! This book is more than just a casual read; it is a valuable resource for teenagers seeking financial independence. We are excited that you have joined us on a financial adventure that will change your life!

REFERENCES

Adams, R. (2023a, October 5). *30 best side hustles for teens*. Wealthup. https://wealthup.com/best-side-hustles-teens/

Adams, R. (2023b, October 10). *Best investing apps for teens [stock apps for under 18]*. Wealthup. https://wealthup.com/best-financial-apps-for-young-adults/

Affordable care act. (2023, May 1). IRS. https://www.irs.gov/affordable-care-act#:

Alamy. (n.d.). *Our top 10 reasons for giving back*. AARP. https://createthegood.aarp.org/volunteer-ideas/reasons-to-give-back.html

Alleyne, C. (2018, November 13). *The easiest ways to give back to your community*. Country Living. https://www.countryliving.com/life/g24995021/giving-back-community/

Ames, M. (2019). *The importance and benefits of giving back to your community*. EF Blog. https://www.ef.com/wwen/blog/efacademyblog/importance-giving-back-to-your-community/

Ashford, K. (2020a, August 12). *What is compound interest?* Forbes Advisor. https://www.forbes.com/advisor/investing/compound-interest/

Ashford, K. (2020b, November 20). *What is cryptocurrency?* Forbes Advisor. https://www.forbes.com/advisor/investing/cryptocurrency/what-is-cryptocurrency/

Average career and job salaries by occupation. (n.d.). Careerprofiles. https://www.careerprofiles.info/salaries.html

Banking basics card game. (2022d, September 1). Consumer Financial Protection Bureau. https://www.consumerfinance.gov/consumer-tools/educator-tools/youth-financial-education/teach/activities/banking-basics-card-game/

Barnes, J. (2019, April 1). *Abundance vs. scarcity — which mindset is yours?* Medium. https://medium.com/@jarrodbarnes/abundance-vs-scarcity-which-mindset-is-yours-5f0149144263

Barysevich, A. (2020, November 20). *How social media influence 71% consumer buying decisions*. Search Engine Watch. https://www.searchenginewatch.com/2020/11/20/how-social-media-influence-71-consumer-buying-decisions/

Beaulieu, A. (2019, December 19). *Why financial emotional intelligence is the predictor of ultimate success*. Forbes. https://www.forbes.com/sites/forbescoachescouncil/2019/12/27/why-financial-emotional-intelligence-is-the-predictor-of-ultimate-success/?sh=7ac20eb650d7

Bennett, R. (2022, October 20). *6 top reasons to save your money*. Bankrate. https://www.bankrate.com/banking/savings/top-reasons-to-save-money/

Berger, R. (2022, May 8). *5 apps to help teens start investing*. Forbes. https://www.forbes.com/sites/robertberger/2022/05/08/5-apps-to-help-teens-start-investing/?sh=33ab69dc5c9e

Berkey-Woodruff (ed.), 11 19. (2018, November 18). *The ethics of giving: Philosophers' perspectives on philanthropy*. Notre Dame Philosophical Reviews. https://ndpr.nd.edu/reviews/the-ethics-of-giving-philosophers-perspectives-on-philanthropy/

Blanchfield, T. (2022, March 24). *How to shift from a scarcity mindset to an abundance mindset*. Verywell Mind. https://www.verywellmind.com/how-to-shift-from-a-scarcity-mindset-to-an-abundance-mindset-5220862

Brown , C. W. (2022, July 18). *8 rules for developing financial discipline*. Brown Miller Wealth Management. https://brownmillerwm.com/8-rules-for-developing-financial-discipline/

Build an emergency fund. (2022, June 29). Investopedia. https://www.investopedia.com/personal-finance/how-to-build-emergency-fund/

Burnette, M. (2023, February 17). *Emergency fund: What it is and why it matters*. NerdWallet. https://www.nerdwallet.com/article/banking/emergency-fund-why-it-matters#:

Bushee, M. (2022, April 21). *Why finance leaders embrace emotional intelligence*. Tipalti. https://tipalti.com/why-finance-leaders-embrace-emotional-intelligences/

Cantin, D. (2022, May 31). *The importance of giving back*. Forbes. https://www.forbes.com/sites/forbesbusinesscouncil/2022/05/31/the-importance-of-giving-back/?sh=667a906e7139

Castrillon, C. (2020, July 20). *5 ways to go from A scarcity to abundance mindset*. Forbes. https://www.forbes.com/sites/carolinecastrillon/2020/07/12/5-ways-to-go-from-a-scarcity-to-abundance-mindset/?sh=43dbfdc1197d

Cherry, K. (2022, January 26). *5 key components of emotional intelligence*. Verywell Mind. https://www.verywellmind.com/components-of-emotional-intelligence-2795438

Cherry, K. (2023, May 2). *Emotional intelligence: How we perceive, evaluate, express, and control emotions*. Verywell Mind. https://www.verywellmind.com/what-is-emotional-intelligence-2795423

Clootrack. (2022). *How does social media influence consumer behavior?* Clootrack. https://www.clootrack.com/knowledge_base/how-does-social-media-influence-consumer-behavior

Cote, C. (2022, July 6). *Why is budgeting important in business? 5 reasons*. Harvard Business School Online. https://online.hbs.edu/blog/post/importance-of-budgeting-in-business

Creating a buying plan. (2022b, June 9). Consumer Financial Protection Bureau. https://www.consumerfinance.gov/consumer-tools/educator-tools/youth-financial-education/teach/activities/creating-buying-plan/?utm_ source=WAT&utm_medium=Art&utm_campaign=FHI360_1809_Art

Creating a savings first aid kit. (2022a, June 2). Consumer Financial Protection Bureau. https://www.consumerfinance.gov/consumer-tools/educator-tools/ youth-financial-education/teach/activities/creating-savings-first-aid-kit/

Credit history definition. (2019). Investopedia. https://www.investopedia.com/terms/ c/credit-history.asp

Cruze, R. (2022, April 25). *How to set financial goals.* Ramsey Solutions. https:// www.ramseysolutions.com/personal-growth/setting-financial-goals

Crypto for teenagers. (n.d.). TeenVestor. https://www.teenvestor.com/crypto-for- teenagers#:~

Darko Jacimovic. (2022, September 7). *25+ educational financial literacy statistics you need to learn about.* MoneyTransfers. https://moneytransfers.com/news/2022/ 09/07/financial-literacy-statistics

DeNicola, L. (2019, April 8). *What is a good credit score?* Experian. https://www. experian.com/blogs/ask-experian/credit-education/score-basics/what-is-a- good-credit-score/

Dore, K. (2020, November 10). The 6 best budgeting apps of 2020. *Investopedia.* https://www.investopedia.com/best-budgeting-apps-5085405

Durana, A. (2023, May 1). *What is investing?* NerdWallet. https://www.nerdwallet. com/article/investing/what-is-investing

Eight types of insurance you can't go without. (2023b, November 7). Ramsey Solutions. https://www.ramseysolutions.com/insurance/types-insurance-cant-go- without

Eliminate financial problems through self discipline. (2013, March 5). Brian Tracy. https://www.briantracy.com/blog/financial-success/eliminate-financial-prob lems-through-self-discipline-financial-independence/

Eneriz, A. (2023, September 15). *Debt avalanche vs. debt snowball: What's the differ- ence?* Investopedia. https://www.investopedia.com/articles/personal-finance/ 080716/debt-avalanche-vs-debt-snowball-which-best-you.asp#:

Explaining 6 key types of retirement plans. (2022, February 19). Americanexpress. https://www.americanexpress.com/en-us/credit-cards/credit-intel/types-of- retirement-plans/

Fay, B. (2012). *Good debt vs. bad debt - types of good and bad debts.* Debt. https://www. debt.org/advice/good-vs-bad/

Fernando, J. (2023, May 18). *The power of compound interest: Calculations and exam- ples.* Investopedia. https://www.investopedia.com/terms/c/compoundinterest. asp#:

Five activities to help you teach your child about money (2020, May 4).

Mothersteachingmoney. https://mothersteachingmoney.com/5-activities-to-help-you-teach-your-child-about-money/

Five ways to build a growth mindset for better money management. (2022, February 24). Northstarfinancial. https://www.northstarfinancial.com/news-events/how-to-have-a-growth-mindset/

Five ways to save for a big purchase. (n.d.). Wsfsbank. https://www.wsfsbank.com/help-guidance/knowledge-center/5-ways-to-save-for-a-big-purchase

Fontinelle, A. (2021, March 29). *Setting financial goals for your future.* Investopedia. https://www.investopedia.com/articles/personal-finance/100516/setting-financial-goals/

Four reasons why you need an emergency fund. (2017, May 8). Banking Topics Blog. https://www.discover.com/online-banking/banking-topics/why-you-need-an-emergency-fund/

Fowler, J. (2021, September 30). *Why an emergency fund is important.* Investopedia. https://www.investopedia.com/financial-edge/0812/why-an-emergency-fund-is-important.aspx

Frankenfield, J. (2023, February 4). *Cryptocurrency explained with pros and cons for investment.* Investopedia. https://www.investopedia.com/terms/c/cryptocurrency.asp

Ganti, A. (2023, April 30). *What is a budget? Plus 10 budgeting myths holding you back.* Investopedia. https://www.investopedia.com/terms/b/budget.asp

Gillespie, L. (2023, June 22). *Bankrate's annual emergency fund report.* Bankrate. https://www.bankrate.com/banking/savings/emergency-savings-report/#key-stats

Glover, L., & Ashford, K. (2022, April 4). *How to choose health insurance: Your step-by-step guide.* NerdWallet. https://www.nerdwallet.com/article/health/choose-health-insurance

Gobel, R. (2023, January 13). *A guide to federal vs private student loans.* Sallie Mae. https://www.salliemae.com/blog/federal-vs-private-student-loans-guide/

Green, R. (2023, February 28). *57% of americans can't cover A $1,000 emergency with savings—here's how you can prepare for unexpected costs and build an emergency fund.* Yahoo Finance. https://finance.yahoo.com/news/57-americans-t-cover-1-140000368.html?guccounter=1#:

Green, S. (2022, March 15). *10 insanely valuable money management tips for teenagers.* Allmomsblog. https://allmomsblog.com/money-management-tips-for-teenagers/

Grossman, A. L. (2019, February 11). *How to teach delayed gratification (exercises for self control).* Money Prodigy. https://www.moneyprodigy.com/how-to-teach-delayed-gratification/

Grossman, A. L. (2021, May 2). *17 money mindset exercises (tools to shift from scarcity to abundance*). Frugal Confessions. https://www.frugalconfessions.com/financial-health/money-mindset-exercises/

Growth mindset vs. fixed mindset: What's the difference? (2023, May 11). Entrepreneur. https://www.entrepreneur.com/leadership/growth-mindset-vs-fixed-mindset-whats-the-difference/450830

Half of American households have no retirement savings. (2023, April 25). USAFacts. https://usafacts.org/data-projects/retirement-savings

Hayes, A. (2023, March 16). *Investment basics explained with types to invest in.* Investopedia. https://www.investopedia.com/terms/i/investment.asp

Hertenstein, I. (2023, January 21). *Young people know more about Tiktok and Minecraft than money.* MarketWatch. https://www.marketwatch.com/story/young-people-know-more-about-tiktok-and-minecraft-than-money-teenagers-want-to-be-smarter-about-finances-teach-them-11674198585

Higuera, V. P. (2023, February 10). *How to set up a savings account for a teenager.* MyBankTracker. https://www.mybanktracker.com/savings/faq/how-to-set-up-a-savings-account-for-a-teenager-297534

Holzhauer, B. (2021, May 26). *The best budgeting apps of june 2021.* Forbes Advisor. https://www.forbes.com/advisor/banking/best-budgeting-apps/

How the debt snowball method works. (2021, April 22). Ramsey Solutions. https://www.ramseysolutions.com/debt/how-the-debt-snowball-method-works

How to invest in cryptocurrency: Beginner's guide. (2023, November 6). Stash. https://www.stash.com/learn/how-to-invest-in-cryptocurrency/

How to maintain a good credit score. (n.d.). Capital One. https://www.capitalone.com/learn-grow/money-management/how-to-maintain-good-credit-score/

How to make a budget: Your step-by-step guide. (2023a, August 24). Ramsey Solutions. https://www.ramseysolutions.com/budgeting/how-to-make-a-budget

How to save up money as a teenager for your next big purchase. (2023). Better Money Habits. https://bettermoneyhabits.bankofamerica.com/en/saving-budgeting/saving-money-as-a-teenager

Huntington. (2022). *Create a personal budget: How to make A budget.* Huntington Bank. https://www.huntington.com/learn/budgeting/how-to-make-a-budget

Irby, L. (2022, July 5). *How to help your teenager build a good credit score.* The Balance. https://www.thebalancemoney.com/help-your-child-build-a-good-credit-score-960520

Islam, R. (2021, May 28). *Research shows you can earn way more money by boosting your emotional intelligence.* The Startup. https://medium.com/swlh/research-shows-you-can-earn-way-more-money-by-boosting-your-emotional-intelligence-934d78c4323e

Kagan, J. (2019). *Credit score.* Investopedia. https://www.investopedia.com/terms/c/credit_score.asp

Kagan, J. (2022, January 3). *Individual retirement account (IRA)*. Investopedia. https://www.investopedia.com/terms/i/ira.asp

Kagan, J. (2023, April 20). *Insurance: Definition, how it works, and main types of policies*. Investopedia. https://www.investopedia.com/terms/i/insurance.asp

Kamat, A. (2021, April 12). *37 money saving tips for teenagers*. Frugal Beat. https://www.frugalbeat.com/money-saving-tips-for-teenagers/?v=68caa8201064

Kaplan, E. (2018, January 16). *EQ can make you wealthy and successful, according to science—here's how to build yours*. CNBC. https://www.cnbc.com/2018/01/16/ceo-elle-kaplan-eq-can-make-you-successful-according-to-science.html

Karr, A. (2023, July 5). *Why It's Important to Save Money at an Early Age*. Mydoh. https://www.mydoh.ca/learn/money-101/money-basics/why-kids-and-teens-should-start-saving-money-early/#:

Keinath, S. (2021, May 20). *Build a bank activity*. 4-H Youth Money Management. https://www.canr.msu.edu/resources/build-a-bank-activity

Kennedy, L. (2021, December 23). *7 ways to achieve financial discipline*. SoFi. https://www.sofi.com/learn/content/achieving-financial-discipline/

Kilroy, A. (2022, May 24). *8 different types of insurance policies and coverage you need*. Forbes Advisor. https://www.forbes.com/advisor/insurance/types-of-insurance-policies/

Kumar, B. (2022, October 29). *How to build a brand in 7 steps: Get started in 2023*. Shopify. https://www.shopify.com/za/blog/how-to-build-a-brand

Library of congress Aesop fables. (2022). Read. https://read.gov/aesop/025.html

Long, J. (2014, December 25). *10 self-made billionaires share the secret to their success*. Business Insider. https://www.businessinsider.com/billionaires-share-secrets-of-success-2014-12

Luthi, B. (2022, October 11). *9 tips for paying off student loans fast*. Bankrate. https://www.bankrate.com/loans/student-loans/repay-college-loans-fast/

Mantilla, S., & CFEI. (2021, June 25). *Fixed mindset vs. growth mindset [yes, it impacts your financial success]*. Money Tamer. https://moneytamer.com/fixed-mindset-vs-growth-mindset/

Marr, J. (2016, March 30). *Switch, by Chip & Dan Heath book summary*. Medium. https://medium.com/@jeffmarr/switch-by-chip-dan-heath-book-summary-b2d72a2944b8#:

Maxabella, B. (2022, April 14). *Delayed gratification is a key to wealth (if you can wait long enough)*. Moneywiseglobal. https://www.moneywiseglobal.com/article/delayed-gratification-is-a-key-to-wealth-if-you-can-wait-long-enough/

McDowell, E. (2023, March 25). *19 famous figures who went from rags to riches*. Business Insider. https://www.businessinsider.com/millionaires-billionaires-who-came-from-nothing-rags-to-riches-stories-2019-7#leonardo-del-vecchio-whose-eyeglasses-empire-makes-ray-bans-and-oakleys-once-lived-in-an-orphanage-3

McMaken, L. (2019). *4 types of insurance everyone needs.* Investopedia. https://www. investopedia.com/financial-edge/0212/4-types-of-insurance-everyone-need s.aspx

McNair, K. (2023, April 11). *53% of americans say they don't have any emergency savings—3 tips to get started.* CNBC. https://www.cnbc.com/2023/04/11/tips-to-build-an-emergency-fund.html

Mejia, Z. (2017, June 17). *How Elon Musk and 2 other highly-successful business leaders stay productive.* CNBC. https://www.cnbc.com/2017/06/17/how-elon-musk-and-3-other-highly-successful-business-leaders-stay-productive.html

Michael Page. (n.d.). *The importance of emotional intelligence in finance.* Michael Page. https://www.michaelpage.co.uk/our-expertise/banking-and-financial-services/ importance-emotional-intelligence-finance

Millar, K. (2020, February 7). *16 delayed gratification exercises, worksheets & activities.* PositivePsychology. https://positivepsychology.com/delayed-gratification-exer cises-worksheets/

Miller, D. (2018, January 31). *Why financial intelligence is so emotional.* Psychology Today. https://www.psychologytoday.com/us/blog/the-human-side-finance/ 201801/why-financial-intelligence-is-so-emotional

Miller, K. (2019, December 30). *What is delayed gratification and how to pass the marshmallow test?* PositivePsychology. https://positivepsychology.com/delayed-gratification/

Mind over money: Develop a smarter money mindset. (2020, January 27). Capital One. https://www.capitalone.com/about/newsroom/2020-capitalone-mindover moneystudytips/?v=1695254400098

Mindset matters: Abundance mindset vs. scarcity mindset. (n.d.). Resources.strategic-coach. https://resources.strategiccoach.com/the-multiplier-mindset-blog/mind set-matters-abundance-mindset-vs-scarcity-mindset

Mitra, M. (2020, November 23). *Meet the teens saving for retirement.* Money. https:// money.com/teenagers-retirement-savings-roth-ira/

Napoletano, E. (2020, July 28). *What is investing? How can you start investing?* Forbes Advisor. https://www.forbes.com/advisor/investing/what-is-investing/

Nguyen, M. and B. (2022, November 14). *Abundance vs. scarcity mindset: Which do you have?* Matt and Briley Nguyen[TM]. https://mattandbrileynguyen.com/abun dance-vs-scarcity-mindset/#:

Nicholson, L., & Shon, S. (2023, November 7). *How to use a credit card: Best practices explained.* LendingTree. https://www.lendingtree.com/credit-cards/articles/ how-use-credit-cards/

Oh, H. (2022, August 11). *These are the best ways for teenagers to save money with (or without) a job.* Seventeen. https://www.seventeen.com/life/school/a40670024/

how-to-save-money-teenager/

O'Neill, B. (2011, August). *Steps toward financial resilience*. Njaes.rutgers.edu. https://njaes.rutgers.edu/sshw/message/message.php?p=Finance&m=194

Opperman, M. (2013, December 30). *Financial goals examples*. Credit.org. https://credit.org/blog/financial-goals-examples/

Patel, L. (2023, May 26). *Crafting an impressive resume: A guide for teenagers*. Tynker Blog. https://www.tynker.com/blog/crafting-an-impressive-resume-a-guide-for-teenagers/

Paulus, N. (2022, August 5). *Americans without health insurance: Statistics & facts*. MoneyGeek. https://www.moneygeek.com/insurance/health/analysis/americans-without-coverage/

Payne, K. (2023a, June 19). *Average savings account balance of americans (2023)*. Time. https://time.com/personal-finance/article/average-american-savings-account-balance/

Payne, K. (2023b, November 16). *Best savings accounts for kids and teens*. Forbes. https://www.forbes.com/advisor/banking/savings/best-savings-accounts-for-kids/

Peetz, J., & Davydenko, M. (2021). Financial self-control strategy use: Generating personal strategies reduces spending more than learning expert strategies. *Journal of Experimental Social Psychology, 97*(1016), 104189. https://doi.org/10.1016/j.jesp.2021.104189

PepsiCo reviews.(n.d.). Glassdoor. https://www.glassdoor.com/Reviews/PepsiCo-Reviews-E522.htm

Picardo, E. (2022, July 22). *Investing explained: Types of investments and how to get started*. Investopedia. https://www.investopedia.com/terms/i/investing.asp

Playing an investment game. (2022c, August 18). Consumer Financial Protection Bureau. https://www.consumerfinance.gov/consumer-tools/educator-tools/youth-financial-education/teach/activities/playing-investment-game/

Pryor, S. (n.d.). *50 community service ideas for families*. Www.signupgenius.com. https://www.signupgenius.com/home/community-service-ideas-families.cfm

Quote by Anne Frank. (n.d.). *A quote from Diary of Anne Frank*. Www.goodreads.com. https://www.goodreads.com/quotes/81804-no-one-has-ever-become-poor-by-giving

Quote by Henry Wheeler Shaw. (n.d.). *Debt therapy on Linkedin*. Www.linkedin.com. Retrieved December 4, 2023, from https://www.linkedin.com/posts/debt-therapy_debtfreelife-planningforyourfuture-tekecontrol-activity-6895269539374882816-vDCi/?trk=public_profile_like_view

Quote by Leslie Tayne. (n.d.). *A quote from Life & Debt*. Www.goodreads.com. Retrieved December 4, 2023, from https://www.goodreads.com/quotes/6564729-budgeting-has-only-one-rule-do-not-go-over-budget

Rawle, T. (2023, September 23). *15 frugal tips that are super easy.* Www.checkcity.com. https://www.checkcity.com/personal-finance/frugal-living-tips

Real leaders: Oprah winfrey and the power of empathy. (2020, March 26). Harvard Business Review. https://hbr.org/podcast/2020/03/real-leaders-oprah-winfrey-and-the-power-of-empathy

Retirement calculator. (n.d.). Ramsey Solutions. https://www.ramseysolutions.com/retirement/retirement-calculator?utm_campaign=connectedJourneys&utm_content=retirement_calc_sharing&utm_term=investing_tax_dfd&utm_source=link_share

Rocke, J. (2023, January 12). *Incorporating growth mindset in personal finance classes.* Edutopia. https://www.edutopia.org/article/growth-mindset-personal-finance/

Rockwood, K. (2020, September 25). *A teen's guide for charitable giving.* Step. https://step.com/money-101/post/a-teens-guide-for-charitable-giving

Rogers, W. (2021, February 10). *25 life-changing money quotes to save more and spend wisely.* Our Mindful Life. https://www.ourmindfullife.com/save-money-quotes/

Royal, J. (2023, August 23). *How to start investing in cryptocurrency: A guide for beginners.* Bankrate. https://www.bankrate.com/investing/how-to-invest-in-cryptocurrency-beginners-guide/

Rubenstein, R. (2016, November 23). *The David Rubenstein Show: Indra Nooyi.* Www.bloomberg.com. https://www.bloomberg.com/news/videos/2016-11-23/the-david-rubenstein-show-indra-nooyi

Saving for a big purchase? Follow these 4 tips. (n.d.). Merrill Edge. https://www.merrilledge.com/life-events/large-purchases/major-purchase

Saving up for a big-ticket item in 2023? Read this first. (2023, January 17). N26. https://n26.com/en-eu/blog/how-to-appraoch-saving-for-something-big

Schwahn, L. (2020, December 18). *What is a budget?* NerdWallet. https://www.nerdwallet.com/article/finance/what-is-a-budget

Schwann, L. (2023, July 18). *Financial goals: Definition and examples.* NerdWallet. https://www.nerdwallet.com/article/finance/financial-goals-definition-examples#:

Securian Financial. (2022). *5 steps to build an emergency fund.* Securian Financial. https://www.securian.com/insights-tools/articles/5-steps-to-building-an-emergency-fund.html

Segal, J., Smith, M., Robinson, L., & Shubin, J. (2023, February 28). *Improving emotional intelligence (EQ).* HelpGuide. https://www.helpguide.org/articles/mental-health/emotional-intelligence-eq.htm

Segal, T. (2023, July 1). *The ins and outs of diversification*. Investopedia. https://www. investopedia.com/terms/d/diversification.asp

Self-Control is the key to growing your finances. (2016, April 26). Avante Financial Services. https://avantefinancial.com.au/grow-financial-self-control/

Six steps to creating an emergency fund. (2022). Morgan Stanley; Morgan Stanley. https://www.morganstanley.com/articles/how-to-build-an-emergency-fund

Six ways to reduce money stress. (n.d.). Fultonbank. https://www.fultonbank. com/Education-Center/Saving-and-Budgeting/6-ways-to-build-financial-disci pline

Skills You Need. (2022). *Choosing the right insurance*. Skillsyouneed. https://www. skillsyouneed.com/num/choosing-insurance.html

Smith, K. A. (2018, August 30). *13 types of cryptocurrency that aren't bitcoin*. Bankrate; Bankrate.com. https://www.bankrate.com/investing/types-of-cryptocurrency/

Speights, K. (2023, August 30). *Warren buffett turns 93 today: Here's his best investing advice ever*. The Motley Fool. https://www.fool.com/investing/2023/08/30/ warren-buffett-turns-93-best-investing-advice-ever/#:~:text=11.

SPENT. (2023). Playspent. https://playspent.org/html/

Swift, E. (2021, October 6). *3 steps to move from a fixed to a growth money mindset*. SUCCESS. https://www.success.com/3-steps-to-move-from-a-fixed-to-a-growth-money-mindset/

Switch. (2013). Heath Brothers. https://heathbrothers.com/books/switch/

Teen spending habits in 2019. (2019, July 26). Lexingtonlaw. https://www.lexington law.com/blog/credit-cards/teen-spending-habits.html

The power of building emotional intelligence into banking experiences. (2022, November 15). Grand Studio. https://www.grandstudio.com/the-power-of-building-emotional-intelligence-into-banking-experiences/

The seven best budget apps for 2021. (2023, November 2). NerdWallet. https://www. nerdwallet.com/article/finance/best-budget-apps

Tips for managing debt. (n.d.). Wellsfargo. https://www.wellsfargo.com/goals-credit/ smarter-credit/manage-your-debt/tips-for-managing-debt/

Turak, A. (2011, November 21). *Steve jobs and the one trait all innovative leaders share*. Forbes. https://www.forbes.com/sites/augustturak/2011/11/21/steve-jobs-and-the-one-trait-all-innovative-leaders-share/?lipi=urn:li:page:d_flag ship3_pulse_read

Turner, T. (2023, November 7). *What does it mean & how does it work?* Annuity. https://www.annuity.org/personal-finance/investing/

Twenty-five ways to make money online and offline. (n.d.). NerdWallet. https://www. nerdwallet.com/article/finance/how-to-make-money

Twenty-three resume tips for 2023. (2023, January 10). Mignone Center for Career Success. https://careerservices.fas.harvard.edu/blog/2023/01/10/23-resume-tips-for-2023/

Types of retirement plans. (2019). U.S. department of labor. https://www.dol.gov/general/topic/retirement/typesofplans

Vaidhya, N. (2019, September 24). *How to plan your retirement from teen age?* LinkedIn. https://www.linkedin.com/pulse/how-plan-your-retirement-from-teen-age-nikhil-vaidhya/

Vamdatt, R. (2020, June 3). *What is a savings account? A simple explanation for kids, teens and beginners.* Easy Peasy Finance for Kids and Beginners. https://www.easypeasyfinance.com/savings-account-for-kids-teens/

Vinnedge, M. (2022, January 1). *9 smart spending and saving tips.* SUCCESS. https://www.success.com/9-smart-spending-and-saving-tips/

Wallace, S. (2022, July 27). *15 charity event ideas that are fun for the whole family.* Www.frontstream.com. https://www.frontstream.com/blog/15-charity-event-ideas

Warren, D., Andalón, M., & Gasser, C. (2019, December). *Shop or save: How teens manage their money.* Growingupinaustralia. https://growingupinaustralia.gov.au/research-findings/annual-statistical-reports-2018/shop-or-save-how-teens-manage-their-money

What is an excellent credit score? (n.d.). Equifax. https://www.equifax.com/personal/education/credit/score/articles/-/learn/what-is-a-credit-score/

What is cryptocurrency and how does it work? (2022). Kaspersky. https://www.kaspersky.com/resource-center/definitions/what-is-cryptocurrency

What is delayed gratification? (n.d.). MBA Financial Strategists. https://www.mbafs.com.au/in-the-news/latest-articles/how-can-delayed-gratification-help-you-with-your-finances/

What is emotional intelligence and how does it apply to the workplace?, 2023). Mental Health America. https://mhanational.org/what-emotional-intelligence-and-how-does-it-apply-workplace

White, A. (2020, January 28). *77% of americans are anxious about their financial situation—here's how to take control.* CNBC. https://www.cnbc.com/select/how-to-take-control-of-your-finances/

White, A. (2021, March 24). *4 questions to ask yourself before making a big purchase.* CNBC. https://www.cnbc.com/select/questions-to-ask-yourself-before-making-a-big-purchase/

Why finance leaders embrace emotional intelligence. (2022, April 21). Tipalti. https://tipalti.com/why-finance-leaders-embrace-emotional-intelligences/

Wikipedia Contributors. (2019, June 8). *Strange case of dr jekyll and mr hyde.* Wikimedia Foundation. https://en.wikipedia.org/wiki/Strange_Case_of_Dr_Jekyll_and_Mr_Hyde

Winfrey, O. (n.d.). *Oprah Winfrey quote: "Leadership is about empathy. it is about having the ability to relate to and connect with people for the purpose of insp...*" Quotefancy. https://quotefancy.com/quote/879880/Oprah-Winfrey-Leadership-is-about-empathy-It-is-about-having-the-ability-to-relate-to-and

Woodly, K. (2023, September 27). *How to save money as a teen [with or without a job, 2023].* Wealthup. https://wealthup.com/best-ways-to-save-money-for-teenagers/

Your credit history. (2012, August 9). Consumer.gov. https://consumer.gov/credit-loans-debt/your-credit-history